UAE 2050: QUANTUM LEAP TO GLOBAL SUPREMACY
THE QUANTUM REVOLUTION

By

Mustafa Nejem

CONTENTS

INTRODUCTION

Let's fast forward and imagine the year is 2050. The United Arab Emirates is a country whose character was changed forever by the tremendous power of quantum management and became one of its unique voices on the world stage. The UAE's journey from early childhood to an economic superpower that is respected for its visionary leaders and technological innovations provides a story of determination, inspiration, and adaptation. Other countries are reactionary to change, while the UAE is proactive as it defines society, economy, and governance through a quantum lens. By emulating the probabilistic nature of quantum phenomena, quantum-inspired policies empower decentralised, adaptive decision-making and cultivate innovative ecosystems. The resulting quantum leap catapulted the nation decades ahead. Today, the pulsating heart of Dubai beats to the rhythm of quantum computing. Hyperloop pods whisk travelers between Abu Dhabi and Sharjah in minutes. And the space elevator to the Mars Science City research colony glints in the sunlight. But above all, it's the enterprising, inclusive, and dynamic spirit of the Emirati people that shines brightest.

Quantum principles may seem complex at first, yet simple truths lie at their core: interconnectivity, collaboration, and embracing change as an opportunity. As we explore the UAE's quantum management revolution through compelling human stories, concrete policies, and technological breakthroughs, these vital lessons become clear. And it is these takeaways that make the UAE's transformative journey relevant for aspiring nations and global leaders worldwide.

Through inspired urban planning, the UAE now boasts sustainable quantum cities where artificial intelligence optimizes energy and transit flows. Meanwhile, Q-fi nano-sensors blanket agricultural lands, enabling extreme precision in water usage. And universities offer cutting-edge quantum education, producing pioneers in quantum computing, cryptography, and bio-engineering.

On the global stage, the UAE's Quantum Diplomacy strengthened ties between nations through cultural exchange and resolving shared challenges. Today, the UAE spearheads humanitarian efforts, leveraging quantum technologies to maximize impact. And the nation's leadership in developing a secure quantum Internet established standards that were emulated worldwide.

The UAE provides living proof that embracing uncertainty and change leads to exponential progress. As the architect of its own quantum leap, the UAE transformed itself from a fledgling federation dependent on pearling and oil to the economic powerhouse and innovation hub we see today.

Looking back, the seeds of the UAE's quantum future were planted decades ago. As early as the 1990s, leaders recognized the nation's overreliance on finite oil reserves. This spurred economic diversification and an emphasis on educating youth. When quantum technologies emerged in the following decades, the UAE already possessed a solid foundation for rapid adaptation.

The UAE's course was further charted through the Vision 2021 and UAE Centennial 2071 plans. The competitive knowledge economy was created by Vision 2021 through education, innovation, and smart infrastructure. However, the UAE Centennial 2071 outlines the next centuries until the UAE teaches about the best nations on earth. Quantum principles enable the realization of this vision. At the government level, the UAE appointed a Minister of State for Quantum Computing to align quantum policies nationwide. And the Emirates Blockchain Strategy 2021 cements the nation as a global leader in blockchain, contributing to quantum readiness.

Meanwhile, building a collaborative quantum ecosystem became key. Business setbacks early on taught the risks of isolated efforts. But then the government, academics, and private sectors united to forge a quantum alliance. Together, they nurtured start-ups through targeted funding programs like the Abu Dhabi Quantum Initiative. And global partnerships, such as with the USA's National Quantum Initiative, brought valuable knowledge exchange.

Embodying the UAE's spirit, Dubai demonstrated the transformative power of quantum principles through its Museum of the Future. The iconic torus structure symbolizes embracing unknowns on the path to greatness. Inside, the museum previews future technologies while promoting proactive and collaborative mindsets. This physical manifestation of the UAE's quantum thinking cements its role as a global nexus for innovation.

The UAE's journey provides a roadmap to the future for other nations while offering invaluable lessons in adaptability, resilience, and quantum thinking. By boldly venturing into the unknown, the UAE achieved astounding progress in a single generation. This living proof gives hope that humanity can overcome any challenge through vision, collaboration, and embracing change as an opportunity.

Chapter 1

Vision of 2050

When we look at the United Arab Emirates today, it's clear this is a nation that dreams big and delivers. The sparkling cityscapes, man-made marvels like Palm Jumeirah, and incredible rise from desert outpost to global hub show the UAE shoots for the stars. Now the leaders have unveiled Vision 2050—an ambitious blueprint declaring the country's aim to become number one in the world within the next quarter century. Spearheaded by His Highness Sheikh Mohammed bin Rashid Al Maktoum, the visionary Vice President and Prime Minister of the UAE and ruler of Dubai, Vision 2050 lays out a vibrant future: By 2050, the UAE will achieve benchmarks from building the planet's best education system to conquering renewable energy to exploring Mars and beyond. Talk about high hopes! But we shouldn't bet against this ambitious nation.

In its first 50 years since unifying seven emirates, the UAE has already exceeded expectations by transforming barren sand into a cosmopolitan oasis brimming with culture. The themes of innovation, openness, and social responsibility ring loudly in Vision 2050. It won't be easy for this dynamic country of some 10 million citizens to hit all its targets amidst a breakneck technological revolution worldwide. However, if any nation can adapt on the fly yet keep the long view, I'd put my money on the UAE to give the top spot a run by 2050.

This chapter gives a friendly rundown of Vision 2050's key goals across areas from the economy to sustainability and beyond that position the UAE to potentially emerge number one globally.

Key Pillars of UAE Vision 2050:

There were many visionary initiatives taken by UAE which has led to the development and enhancement of their economy. Following are some of the key pillars that align with the success of United Arab Emirates. By following these initiatives and the strategies, it will lead to success in the modern world.

- Economic diversification has led to the success and boost in their economy.
- UAE is also focusing on investing in renewable energy sources, non oil technologies and knowledge based industries. This has helped them in reducing the dependence on oil based technology.
- Additionally, UAE has also focused on the importance of research, development, and innovation which has enhanced the competitiveness in the global market and increased the economic growth.

Economic Growth:

Through economic diversification and boosting the GDP, the UAE has elevated economic growth. UAE is involved in the expansion of nonoil technology. Also, it is indulged in more tourism activities and knowledge-based sectors. UAE has created a very innovative business environment for international investments. UAE is now a preferable destination for international businesses as compared to other countries. It has created a great working environment by hiring skilled workers. It has a diverse workforce that is skilled in multiple tasks.

This workforce has been created by the big businesses in UAE through the conduction of different educational programs and professional development sessions, which has created a more dynamic society. It is now indulged in developing new economic factors. It has invested in the space industry, comprising space technology, satellites, and other techniques to be number one in the global space industry. UAE is also expanding their renewable energy projects.

For example, the Barakah Nuclear Power Plant is the first power plant that is constructed by United Arab Emirates. It is situated in the Dhafra region and comprises 4 nuclear reactors. This plant uses PWR Technology for generating electricity. The main purpose of this project by UAE is to diversify the energy sources. This will help the UAE reduce its dependence on fossil fuels, gas, and oil. This Barakah power plant aims to provide sustainable development in the UAE by minimizing the numerous greenhouse gas emissions. Additionally, it helps the UAE to become the number one country in the world for nuclear energy capabilities. It will also lead the UAE to International partnerships and collaborations.

Another example is Mohammed Bin Rashid Al Maktoum Solar Park is located in Dubai. It is one of the largest solar parks in the world. This project is set by UAE which will give fruitful results in the future. This Park includes CSP Technology which helps store energy. It plays a central role in the commitment of the UAE to move towards renewable energy sources. It also reduces the reliance on fossil fuels. The Solar Park is considered a hub for solar technology innovation. The construction of this Solar Park will create more job opportunities which will stimulate economic growth. Additionally, this Park attracts the renewable energy sector for investments as well which will foster a dynamic economy.

Emphasizing Education:

UAE has learned the fact that by emphasizing innovation and education they can have long-term success. So they have developed many world-class education systems that have enhanced the infrastructure and development of education according to global standards. UAE has also invested in skilled and professional features technology and research facilities for the students which helps in fostering partnerships with international institutions.

This helps in a great educational exchange between different countries. It will also involve in establishing research and development centers for creating more innovative technology. Now it is also clear in focusing on the future skills for a more robust growth. UAE has a great interest in developing specialized programs and taking initiative in new fields. UAE has also foster many innovation hubs for creating a dynamic learning environment.

The main example set by the UAE for promoting education Is the promotion of STEM education for the future. This will help in cultivating a workforce that will be prepared for various opportunities and challenges in the future. It comprises professionals from the Science, Technology, Engineering, and Mathematics fields which will be addressing all the challenges associated with these fields in UAE. It will enhance the competitiveness of UAE in the global market which will foster technology advancements and innovation. This will be done with the help of a skilled workforce and be experienced in STEM disciplines. This will help in addressing various challenges and will contribute to scientific advancements at the global level. Another example includes the *National Higher Education Strategy 2030*. This strategy is adopted by UAE which aims to shape the higher education system of UAE according to the world standards. It refers to innovation, development of knowledge, and economic diversification. According to this education strategy, the UAE is hoping to get the desired results in the field of innovation and research. It will also nurture culturally and socially responsible students which will help in the development of an inclusive society.

Community Cohesion and Happiness:

By building a happy community, the UAE can lead to the enhancement of the overall well-being of any society. It has always promoted cultural awareness in the people to strengthen the identity of any community. UAE has also encouraged social communication through cultural exchange, festivals events, and community gatherings. Nowit has also invested in numerous fruitful initiatives that will foster a sense of belonging among all the residents of any specific society. It also emphasize tolerance which is essential for a successful environment.

It is done by them through public awareness programs, campaigns, and educational sessions by implementing different policies for tolerance and inclusion. Human rights will highly be protected and it will also promote equal opportunities for all the people living in the same society. The main aim of UAE professionals is to prioritize the mental health initiative as well. This will help in enhancing the overall comfort and happiness of the people by investing in the healthcare departments and services that ensure a quality medical checkup for all the people.

This helps in developing a sustainable and healthy environment in different cities of UAE. UAE is also focusing on numerous social services. It is also trying to develop many standardized techniques for measuring the level of happiness in different communities. A data-driven technique is used for regulating the happiness levels that contribute to the overall well-being of society. It will also encourage the participation of individuals in different tasks. So by prioritizing tolerance and community cohesion, the UAE can create a harmonious society in 2050. It will not only prioritize the well-being of the individuals but also enhance the life quality and global position

Infrastructure and Governance:

By developing a great infrastructure and proficient governance, the UAE can increase in terms of growth and sustainability. UAE is investing in many modern emerging transportation systems. They also utilize different technologies for streamlining government processes. This also helps them in improving the delivery of different services. By implementing the e-government initiative through different digital platforms, UAE the is rising in terms of both technology and economy. UAE is practicing more to foster accountability and transparency in all government-related operations. It has previously prioritized mainly public safety. This has been done through advanced security systems.

UAE is implementing many sustainable practices for a great environmental effect. Moreover, for the future, they are integrating numerous smart technologies including waste reduction, energy efficiency management, and as a result the overall efficient management of the country. Different innovations are developed by the UAE for governance-related operations. This will lead to continuous and rapid improvement in the government industry in 2050.

The main example of infrastructure development in the UAE is the Etihad Rail Project. This is a great initiative taken by the UAE to connect numerous industrial areas and cities across the country. It is an efficient railway network that will help in enhancing the goods and passengers movement. The main aim of this transport expansion project in UAE is to create an integrated and modern transportation system that will help in addressing the future needs of the country. This Railway Project will also improve the efficient transport of goods to different cities of the country.

Another notable example is the Space Exploration Hub by UAE which aims to lead the country to the top in the field of space technology. It also helps in fostering collaboration with international space companies and agencies. The main purpose of this space exploration hub is to inspire future generations in the field of science and space exploration.

Challenges and Competition:

There are many challenges and competition that are faced by many developing countries. UAE has faced numerous regional challenges after which it has made many strategies to overcome these challenges which has led to a big economic sector in the world. Right now by 2050, it is hoping to be an even more big market by overcoming all the market competition and sustainability issues.

- **Stiff Regional Competition:**

UAE is conducting a comprehensive analysis of the market to understand its strengths and weaknesses. This will help them in competing among different nations. Is has also adopted a strategic positioning by developing clear and transparent strategies to set UAE fup or regional competition. UAE is also seeking to explore new industries that match the strength and vision of the UAE. It is also diversifying their economy to eliminate their dependency on numerous traditional industries.

UAE has previously strengthened many parts of their economic infrastructure and now they are strengthening more diplomatic collaborations with other international countries. It is seeking more partnerships with different successful countries to increase the presence of the UAE in the competitive market. Additionally, many new policies have been implemented to attract international talented people.

It is establishing more initiatives for promoting collaboration with global professionals. Also by developing accurate and professional branding strategies, UAE can showcase its services and offerings internationally. It will help in increasing global visibility by leveraging numerous International events and digital platforms.

- **Sustainability Issues:**

UAE is addressing sustainability issues very effectively. It is balancing the environmental growth and different environmental factors that have a great impact on the economy of the UAE. It is implementing more green infrastructure which will minimize environmental pollution. It is expected that they will be developing more green spaces, energy-efficient systems, efficient public transport, and eco-friendly architectures for a good living environment. Many strategies for renewable energy resources are also conducted by them to reduce their dependency on traditional fossil fuels.

So by 2050, the UAE is expected to be successful in terms of technology and renewable energy because they are investing in wind energy, solar energy, and other sustainable energy options. Similarly, it is also implementing many efficient strategies for water management. Water recycling and desalination are the prominent techniques and strategies that are used by them to gain future benefits for the country. Additionally, waste management is also one of the crucial steps that must be taken by any country to increase its economy and streamline operations.

So UAE is developing robust waste management systems. This will help them manage the waste and recycle it for more efficient solutions. UAE has previously invested in many technologies and now they are investing more in research and development for smooth practices and modern technology. This will help the initiatives and startups to support sustainable innovation and get a great standing position by 2050.

Thus, by adopting all these strategies and techniques UAE is working to get rapid growth in its economy and a sustainable environment. This ensures that the future of UAE is hopefully brighter and successful because of their innovations and strategies.

Real-Life Examples and Incidents:

Following are some real life examples associated with the vision of UAE for 2050.

- **Abraham Accords:**

Abraham Accords has made a historic achievement for UAE in 2020. This agreement helped normalize the relationships between Bahrain and Israel, which as a result fostered economic collaboration. After establishing these diplomatic relationships, the UAE started work for shipping the Geo politics of the Middle East. So these Abraham Accords were not only promoting peace but also were the main source of cooperation in the healthcare, tourism, and technology sectors.

- **Jebel Ali Free Zone:**

The establishment of this free zone is also a notable example of the visionary journey of the UAE. The main aim of the zone was to attract international collaborations and foreign Investments. This was done by offering foreign businesses, tax incentives, which helped in streamlining the regulations. After the success of this Jebel Ali Free Zone, Dubai was transformed into a business hub globally. This helps them promote the job creation, economic development, diversification, and technology transfers. So this free zone plays a vital role in enhancing the UAE economy without oil dependence.

These examples depict the multifaceted journey of the UAE. UAE has started its journey from economic innovation through the establishment of free zones. This has led to an increase in global progress and impact.

Overall, UAE is adopting numerous efficient strategies and overcoming many challenges regarding the enhancement of its economy. It is diversifying it's economy and managing all the sustainability issues for a better future for the country. Many challenges have been addressed and some are to be improved to increase the attraction of the UAE in the global market. It is prioritizing more on community building, promoting education, and developing smart technologies and energy-efficient solutions which will help foster their economy and will give them positive results by 2050.

CHAPTER 2

THE EMERGENCE OF QUANTUM MANAGEMENT

In an era of exponential technological change, global interconnectivity, and deep uncertainty, traditional business practices appear inadequate to navigate the complexity faced by 21st century organizations. A revolutionary new management methodology is emerging in response—one which embraces the principles of modern physics while catalyzing enterprise, ingenuity and leadership dexterity across spheres of human endeavor from commerce to governance. Its name: Quantum Management.

At first glimpse, Quantum Management may seem counterintuitive to established models that rely on hierarchy, standardization and detailed strategic plans. Instead, it draws inspiration from quantum physics, where particle behaviors seem strange compared to the visible world though with immense latent potential. Similarly, viewing an organization as an interconnected, energetic organism unlocks possibilities stifled by rigid divisions.

Leaders adopting a Quantum mindset cultivate a culture of inquiry, experimentation and informed risk-taking. They understand that in a complex context characterized by multiplying unknowns and exponential change rates, static solutions grow outdated fast. Thus, rather than striving for elusive predictability, managers encourage exploration and learning powered by diversity and collaborative friction incubating breakthrough concepts. With its embrace of system-level thinking, dynamism, and unlocking latent human ingenuity across organizations, Quantum Management may form the foundations for more adaptive leadership paradigms across both private and public sector institutions.

The following overview takes a deeper look at the theories behind Quantum Management as well as real-world examples of how organizations are applying its principles.

Quantum Management Fundamentals:

Following are some of the fundamentals of quantum management that lead to prosperous leadership:

Embracing Uncertainty:

Embracing uncertainty is one of the most essential aspects of the business world. It involves probability and assessments for making different types of decisions in a business organization. For example, a Quantum management approach can be adopted which involves strategic planning where the leaders focus on the potential future and develop a roadmap and strategies for different future scenarios.

Adaptive Leadership:

Adaptive leadership always involves facilitating the individuals working in an organization and guiding them without showing any control or charge over them. Because the leaders are the main part of an organization that adopts different approaches for different emergencies. As a result, this helps in building a learning environment and adaptation.

For example, Dubai Future Foundation is an initiative that uses an attentive decision approach, this Dubai Future Foundation also supports many other programs including the Dubai Future Accelerators Program, where government officials collaborate with different companies to address business challenges.

Inclusive Innovation:

This fundamental of quantum management helps in recognizing the inclusivity value which helps in promoting innovation. Along with this, it also helps in embracing diversification with different perspectives and ideas.

For example, the Accessabilities Expo is an initiative taken by the UAE. This initiative will help in the future for UAE to bring innovation and address the needs of different disabled individuals. It is designed to be easily accessible by different types of people. Moreover, it helps in accommodating individuals with different sensory and physical abilities which ensures an inclusive environment. Additionally, this Expo also serves as a platform for showcasing numerous innovations and technologies designed by the UAE to enhance the lifestyle of disabled people.

Decision Making:

Through decentralized decision-making in any organization, UAE is empowering the teams to make their specific decisions. The most notable example of decentralized decision-making is the vision of the United Arab Emirates for a free zone model. For this, they have designed Dubai Internet City, which is a technology-invented Park. It operates independently while providing different companies with a business environment. Moreover, it allows for flexible regulations which are used to encourage business growth and enhance innovative techniques.

So this Dubai Internet City can help businesses in making rapid decisions without approvals from central authorities. It is a fast-paced technology where emerging technology and adaptation to the latest market trends are very important. Moreover, it also offers numerous services for companies. This approach enables different businesses to select the services that go well with their strategies leading to a powerful business environment.

Global Landscape of Management:

There are numerous traditional models of management in the UAE that are struggling to make a prosperous future. Mostly traditional management follows a hierarchical structure which helps in a continuous flow of work from the top management to various management levels. For example in UAE, many government entities are operated traditionally by the decisions that are made by higher officials and are passed on to the lower levels.

Secondly, the command and control model is also essential in emphasizing the control of the employees of the company and their activities through streamlined processes. For example, some traditional companies in the UAE adhere to the control and command approach. In this approach, the managers observe the production and direct each step to the lower-level staff.

Apart from these two, the bureaucratic model is the third one that plays a major role in Quantum Management. In this model, the bureaucratic management mainly depends on the procedures, rules, and regulations that are fixed which lead to a streamlined and smooth organizational structure. For example, numerous government departments in the UAE follow this bureaucratic model and are characterized by numerous standardized processes.

Along with the benefits of traditional models in UAE, as discussed above, there are some limitations as well. Talking about the limitations of these models, the hierarchical structure can also result in slow and steady processes mainly in large organizations. So by following the hierarchical model, the UAE can lead to slow decision-making and response to changing market trends. Another limitation of the traditional model includes inflexible Bureaucracy. This is because the bureaucratic structures can lead to inflexibility as well which will have a big impact on bureaucratic rigidity.

Real-Life Organisations and Countries Facing Management Challenges:

Many real-life countries and organizations examples are facing many big challenges because of the rigid management of the business models. Following are some of the real-life examples that should be considered for getting an insight into the necessity of smooth Quantum Management.

- **Nokia:**

As we all know Nokia was once a leading organization dealing in mobile phones. However, it has faced numerous challenges because of its rigid management structure which caused it to not adhere to the fast changes in the smartphone market. The lack of agility in this company has resulted in a decline in the market share.

- **Soviet Union:**

The Soviet Union is a country that has followed a bureaucratic and centralized management structure. However, this traditional model has hindered numerous economic technologies and innovations according to market demands. Moreover, this rigid structure comprising of smooth flow of commands from higher to lower levels has finished the individual creativity and ideas. As a result, this contributed to economic inefficiency and the collapse of the Soviet economy.

- **Eastern Kodak:**

Kodak is another organization that is a big leader in photography. But it has also faced many challenges. It has struggled through its rigid management structure which the organization has resulted in very negative consequences in the photography market. This traditional management structure has caused the company to collapse and has also highlighted the effects of inflexible management.

Quantum Management in UAE:

The application of quantum management principles in the UAE reflects a very innovative approach. It also aligns with the vision of UAE for the future. UAE has a very agile approach to governance which is characterized by decision making, policy implementation, and adaptation to changing market trends. For example, the response of the UAE government to COVID 19 has demonstrated its strategies, policy adjustments, rapid communication, and technology usage for robust decision-making.

Secondly, the UAE has also promoted the diverse perspectives of different individuals and has encouraged the participation of all the people at different levels of decision-making.

For example, an initiative by the UAE named as Gender Balance Council has shown the commitment of UAE officials to inclusive leadership. It has helped the government to encourage gender diversity that balances with the quantum management principles.

Quantum Management in Business:

The quantum management principles are highly integrated in the business sector of UAE. This is done to encourage innovation, analyze, and increase adaptability. It involves changing from hierarchical models to technology-driving models. One of the most notable examples of this is the Dubai Blockchain Strategy. This Dubai blockchain strategy tells about strategies for a decentralized economy.

As we all know blockchain helps in eliminating the intermediary's need, which helps in increasing the transparency in transactions. The businesses that are adopting this blockchain strategy are getting benefits in terms of reduced scams, enhanced transparency, and increased efficiency aligning with the different Quantum management decision-making principles.

Quantum Management in Crisis Response:

UAE has suffered from major ill effects of the COVID-19 pandemic. In this time, it has exhibited decision-making strategies for adapting to the current circumstances. It has implemented numerous dynamic principles and measures including travel restrictions, lockdowns, and COVID testing strategies for gathering real-time data and analysis of infection rates. Moreover, it has also built collaboration with numerous government sectors, the health industry, and the technical sector to work in collaboration to get out of this situation. UAE started an initiative known as the National Disinfection Program, which has highlighted strategic approaches and diverse expertise that help to gain positive responses.

Furthermore, there was another campaign that was led by UAE named "Stay Home, Stay Safe", which has also provided support to different businesses and startups. This dynamic approach has focused on public health while considering the economic conditions. So the response of the UAE to the COVID-19 pandemic has reflected the application of Quantum Management in crises by adapting to the changing complexities of health crises globally.

Quantum Management in Innovation Ecosystem:

UAE has adopted many innovations for a better future. For example, the use of AI strategy by the UAE serves as a great roadmap that helps promote artificial intelligence in numerous economic factors. It works with quantum management principles and provides a straight pathway for getting adaptive responses and overcoming challenges. This artificial intelligence strategy has also collaborated with numerous academies, industries, and government sectors to promote an innovative approach.

This is because the quantum management principles mainly emphasize collaboration and interconnectedness which ensures this perspective from diverse individuals in the implementation of artificial intelligence technology. Moreover, the UAE also collaborates at the international level with AI experts which helps in promoting a global perspective for the advancement of artificial intelligence in the UAE.

Real-Life Examples and Incidents:

- **Business Success through Quantum Management:**

Quantum management has effectively caused positive results in different businesses regarding adaptability and growth. The most common example of quantum management in the business sector includes Emirates NBD. It is one of the largest banks in the UAE which has used numerous methodologies for transforming decision-making processes. This transformation has enabled the bank to respond to the changing market trends and improve the customer experience. It has also enhanced the adaptability to changing financial conditions.

This Emirates NBD has adopted a decentralized decision-making policy for empowering different teams. This approach has helped them in rapid problem-solving and enhanced innovative techniques which have led to sustainable growth. So the journey of Emirates NBD showcases the complementation of numerous Quantum management principles which has led to Rapid growth in the financial landscape globally.

- **Innovation Initiative and Collaboration:**

UAE has taken many initiatives to foster innovation through the application of quantum management principles. The main example of this is the Dubai Future Accelerators program. This is a platform that is designed for collaborating with different academies, government officials, and other industries to drive Innovation. Furthermore, it also focuses on problem-driving strategies where government officials give challenges and take innovative solutions from different startup companies. It is done to increase agility, concentration, and diversification for dynamic problem-solving.

Quantum Leadership in Action:

Sheikh Mohammed bin Rashid Al Maktoum is the prime minister of the UAE and head of Dubai. He has promoted adaptive governance through his outstanding leadership skills. Like in the global financial crisis, he has responded very strategically. He has showcased many Quantum leadership principles for adapting to changing economic challenges.

Furthermore, he has also started an initiative known as the Mohammed bin Rashid Al Maktoum Global Initiative which has focused mainly on community development, promotion of healthcare, and education. This has reflected the commitment to quantum leadership strategies for enhancing the skills of different individuals. Moreover, he also engages in international collaborations in which numerous events are hosted by him. These events include the Dubai Future Accelerators program, World Government Summit, etc for demonstrating a strategic approach to embrace economic changes.

As concluded, the examples of UAE applying quantum management provide great insight and understanding of the UAE strategic initiative through the emergence of Quantum Management principles in different fields. The commitment of the UAE to Quantum Management is also exemplified by known leaders, organizations, companies, and other initiatives for embracing an interconnected approach. As we move on to the next chapter, we will be getting information regarding the journey of the UAE in adopting Quantum management principles. We will be exploring numerous challenges, and how Quantum management principles help in shaping the position of the landscape.

Chapter 3

A JOURNEY FROM
SAND TO SKY

Beneath the timeless dunes of UAE, an embarking transformative journey is recorded from deserts to sky heights. Metaphorically, this journey from sand to sky shows the transformation of the United Arab Emirates. The arid deserts of UAE are symbolized by sand from where UAE has risen to new heights encompassing modernity, progress, and prosperity which is represented as the sky. So this metaphor tells you about the remarkable journey of UAE to become a dynamic society and progress more for the future.

Talking about the historic era, the UAE economy was mainly dependent on traditional industries. So at that time, the communities started earning their living through agriculture or crop cultivation. They relied on falcons and other vegetables which served as a major economic activity. So these practices were very helpful in shaping the infrastructure of the UAE societies and the lives of people living there. Moreover, trade also played a very important role at that time mainly in Dubai which served as a strategic location for trading.

Moreover considering trading, cultural practices were very common at that time including pottery, traditional crafts, and weaving. They mainly emphasize on community building and hospitality. As a result, this historic era was known because of its interconnectedness between the people living there and the land, due to which this era laid a foundation of cultural heritage which has influenced the economy of UAE today.

Oil Discovery, An Economic Transformation:

Talking about the economic transformation, the discovery of oil and its resources is evident. Through the discovery of oil in 1960, at that time the production of oil brought a rapid shift in the economy of UAE. This story begins with the continuous efforts of international oil companies that have identified the oil reservoirs in the UAE. As this oil production started, the UAE experienced a very fast growth in their economy. It has also transformed the urban society of the UAE into an industrialized and modern nation. This oil became a very precious and life-changing opportunity for them. It was used in numerous construction activities, educational institutions, modern cities, etc.

Through this, Dubai which was the center for trade and economic growth became a global business hub that symbolizes economic growth. Furthermore, urbanization was also exceeded because of this oil discovery. It has led the UAE to the skylines in transforming their architecture and settlements. Consequently, it results in improvements in the education sector, healthcare, and other daily living needs.

Visionary Leadership:

When talking about visionary leadership in UAE, Sheikh Zayed bin Sultan Al Nayan is a great leader to consider. He has changed the entire architecture of the UAE which plays a very essential role in shaping the trajectory of the UAE. Being the first president of UAE, the leadership of Sheikh Zayed is known for his profound vision for a prosperous nation. He has the main aim of building unity among all the seven emirates by ignoring all the regional and tribal differences. Moreover, he has played a major role in encouraging the utilization of oil for economic development. He was known for his social welfare works by investing mainly in healthcare and education. This is because, under his guidance, the UAE has succeeded in various factors. It has impressed tolerance and inclusivity. He also has a great vision for a harmonious society which has led to the development of modern UAE. Additionally, he focused on sustainable development which promotes the preservation of the natural resources of UAE for the future. Sheikh Zayed Al Nahyan's Legacy is evident from his visions for the UAE which has helped the UAE gain a strong position and prosperity.

Social and Cultural Evolution:

UAE is undergoing remarkable evolution in terms of both culture and society. It has worked mainly for education by investing in numerous academic institutions and educational programs, which have transformed the lives of many people. For example, an initiative named Moral Education focuses on the value of empathy and tolerance. It helps in making individuals forward thinking and shape their lives in a very beautiful manner.

Additionally, women's empowerment is also a main factor of consideration by UAE which has reflected the traditional norms. Because of this, women in the UAE easily participate in numerous sectors including business, education, government, and economy. This also highlights the importance of gender equality and considers women the main contributors to the development of the nation. This cultural advancement reflects a very forward-thinking approach that shows modernity in the UAE heritage.

Economic Diversification:

Considering the economic diversification, the UAE has made new strategies and policies for it. The most common example is JAFZA, Jebel Ali free zone. It was constructed in 1985 and is considered one of the fastest free zones in the UAE. It is a source of providing businesses and attracting numerous diverse industries. This helps in reducing the dependency of the UAE on oil revenue.

Secondly, Dubai International Financial Centre, DIFC is also a leading free zone that is known for its insurance and asset management. It has a strategic framework that follows international standards and helps the UAE become a global financial destination. This initiative helps the UAE economy become more vibrant and robust in the financial sector. Both these initiatives and policies exemplify the proactive approach of the United Arab Emirates for economic diversification. It mainly emphasizes the development of free zones.

Through all these strategies and initiatives, the UAE has reduced its reliance on oil and has built a diversified economy.

Infrastructure Development:

Considering the transportation and infrastructure in UAE, numerous projects are started and also going on for a prosperous future for UAE. Among all Dubai Metro is one of the notable and very beneficial examples of the transportation infrastructure in UAE. This Dubai Metro is an iconic example of the commitment of the UAE to the transportation infrastructure by using different technologies. It is one of the most efficient and rapid metro systems which work globally. It connects numerous areas of Dubai and reduces traffic congestion. Secondly, another example includes Etihad Rail, which is an outstanding railway network project. This was made to connect different cities and industrial areas of UAE. It is not completed yet the work on it has been started. But it will serve as a great project for passenger transportation in the future. This will help in increasing the economic development of the UAE in 2050 and will lead to better connectivity between different areas of the UAE.

Communication Infrastructure:

Along with the transportation infrastructure, the communication infrastructure has also played a big role. UAE has also made advancements technically in the communication sector. For this, the most notable example is the development of Fiber Optic Networks. The United Arab Emirates has invested a big amount for fiber optic networks which are high in speed. They help in facilitating the communication between different cities and areas. It also supports the digital position of the UAE for the future in terms of innovation and technology.

Another main example of communication infrastructure is 5G Technology implementation which has led to a more faster communication. It helps in increasing the advancements in numerous sectors like healthcare, transportation, education, etc. All these transportation and communication infrastructure developments that are started by the UAE will foster connectivity, economic growth, and sustainable technology in the future UAE. This is all the result of the strategic planning and execution of all the projects which will help in making UAE a global player in terms of infrastructure development.

Sustainable Practices:

UAE is mainly focused on increasing the sustainability of the region. For this, they have started many renewable energy projects. The primary example of this is Masdar City, which is a notable sustainable project by the UAE. It is constructed in Abu Dhabi, which is an efficient Urban Development. It comprises numerous renewable energy sources and is built on an energy-efficient design. This will create a low-carbon community in 2050 for UAE

Secondly, the UAE has also invested in solar energy. For example, Mohammed bin Rashid Al Maktoum Solar Park is a common example, which emphasizes the commitment to clean, safe, and affordable energy. It comprises both the CSP and PV technology.

Now considering the Wildlife conservation projects by the UAE, there are numerous initiatives taken in this regard. Notably, Arabian Oryx conservation is more in demand. It is conserved through many breeding techniques and it's habitat restoration. This project for wildlife conservation has shown its dedication to preserving biodiversity. It will also bring many new opportunities for wildlife conservation in the future.

Another initiative, Hawk Release Programs was started, including the International Fund for Houbara Conservation, which has a main emphasis on Houbara Bustard conservation. It is a migratory bird, which is conserved through releasing birds and breeding in their habitats.

Furthermore, sustainable Practices by the UAE also involve many green initiatives. UAE has started many green energy efficient projects including Estidama Pearl Rating System, which is based in Abu Dhabi. The main goal of this project is to analyze the condition of buildings in Abu Dhabi according to their ecological footprint. This is increasing environmental responsibility by promoting energy-efficient systems. So, this multi-faceted approach by the UAE for environmental sustainability helps in embracing economic development and environmental stability.

Technological Advancements:

UAE is committing to numerous technology innovations. This is exemplified by their main Mars Mission. It is also known as Hope Probe, which was launched in 2020. The main aim of this project is to explore the atmosphere of Mars which will have a great impact on the scientific economy globally. For this mission, UAE is equipped with numerous instruments to analyze and collect data on the atmosphere on Mars, which will provide valuable insight into the weather patterns on the planet.

Another notable example of technological advancement in the UAE is the construction of Smart Cities. The smart Dubai initiative helps transform the normal city into a technology-built area. It has a smart infrastructure comprising smart buildings, transportation systems, energy-efficient solutions, etc. It helps in the betterment of the quality of the residents. This integration of new technology goes to governors as well. Numerous equipment services help in smooth processes for the citizens. As a result, it contributes to a more responsive administration. So considering all these initiatives by UAE, It is making many advancements in the scientific sector to prepare the nation to become a technologically advanced country.

Vision 2050: A Continuation:

UAE has made a very remarkable journey in its history. From this journey, you can get insights regarding the foundation of the framework UAE has made for Vision 2050. This vision is mainly for the sustainable development of the nation and its prominence globally. Vision 2050 mainly relies on the legacy of visionary leaders of the UAE who have laid the foundation for the UAE's success. They had a high commitment to proactive governance which is evident from the example of Sheikh Zayed Bin Sultan Al Nahyan. He has ensured long-term goals for the success of the UAE Nation. Moreover, they also had a great emphasis on economic diversification which serves as the foundation for Vision 2050. Now UAE is recognising the need for adapting to modern global changes to build a knowledge-based economy.

For example, UAE has worked on numerous past initiatives like Dubai Future Foundation and Dubai Smart City. It has laid a big foundation for economic growth, sustainable development, and societal advancement. Many green energy and renewable energy initiatives are also taken to make the UAE's future more bright and sustainable. Furthermore, the UAE is also engaged in numerous global affairs and collaborations with other global nations. Because of this, UAE Vision 2050 mainly relies on interconnectedness and international partnerships which will drive mutual success.

So by considering all these historical successes and overcoming all the challenges, vision 2050 can progress in the UAE journey. It mainly depends on the determination, continuity, and innovative capacity to ensure the UAE's development.

Talking about the transformative journey of UAE, we have got a huge information regarding the evolution of this nation from oil dependency to a dynamic global nation. All the historical context highlights the adaptive strategies, innovative techniques, and vision of UAE to become the world's number one country. This chapter has provided insights regarding economic diversification, infrastructure development, sustainable practices, energy-efficient models, and international collaborations.

There are numerous initiatives taken by the UAE including free zones, infrastructure project, and tourism strategies which has played an essential role in reducing the dependency on oil. The quantum management principles have been adopted by this nation along with the forward-thinking strategies and policies that have helped in increasing its economic growth.

Chapter 4

QUANTUM MANAGEMENT:
THE UAE'S UNIQUE APPROACH

Quantum Management in UAE unique approach: Quantum management has laid the foundations of UAE success. It is one of the basics of the social economic strategy adopted by UAE. It helps in the exploration how UAE has used the quantum management principles in fostering innovation, technology and resilience regarding this Quantum Management. UAE has adopted a very unique approach for redefining the pathway and roadmap of nation for success in future. Additionally, the quantum management principles are also adopted by UAE in the field of governance, which helps in promoting sustained growth in future. From visionary leadership to adaptive strategies, you will be getting a distinctive idea of shaping the future of UAE with efficient management principles.

Quantum Management in UAE:

The quantum management in UAE helps in government sector in collaborating internationally. Unlike the traditional management systems, this Quantum management comprise of linear structures which helps in providing a dynamic and interconnected system. In this regard, Quantum Management comprise of a proactive approach and strategy for responsive decision making.

It uses cutting edge technology, responsive methodology and real time analytics for navigating the complexities of governance to evolve in a global landscape. Furthermore, this Quantum Management is also characterized by the emphasize on learning and adaptation. It mainly works on collaboration which fosters interdisciplinary cooperation. This approach helps in making connections with international sectors which promotes responsive ecosystem.

The Fusion of Tradition and Innovation:

The fusion of innovative Quantum Management strategies and the traditional values in UAE gives an insight to a unique synergy. It helps in increasing the strength of both the traditional and the innovative world. At its base, Quantum Management involves a big balance between Innovation and the cultural foundations.

- **Cultural Alignment:**

Quantum Management strategies are adopted in UAE for aligning with the rich culture of the nation. It has a big impact on the traditional values such as respect, truth, loyalty and community which integrates numerous positive decision making processes. It ensures that all these modernization policies are a base of culture of UAE which helps in sense of continuity.

- **Holistic Development:**

The traditional values mostly focus on the holistic and community development. But the quantum management principles mainly focus on the social economic development with a holistic approach. This approach helps in ensuring the societal well being while aligning with the traditional norms and values.

- **Leadership:**

Quantum Management also acknowledges the importance of leadership in the traditions and culture of UAE. The fusion of tradition and innovation comprise of visionary leadership with the quantum management principles where numerous leaders of UAE have inspired innovation. This leadership synthesis helps in maintaining the cultural diversity and also increases adaptability and forward thinking.

Decision Making Processes:

UAE has a tradition of consultation which comprise of quantum management principles. The decision making principles involved in the UAE tradition are inclusive and comprise of diverse perspectives. All these perspectives aligns with the cultural values of inclusive decision making for UAE.

This blend of innovation and culture provides information regarding the UAE commitment to progress in future. It is on the way of success without ignoring its cultural roots by using the quantum management principles with the traditional cultures. UAE is navigating for a good balance between heritage and innovation. It will be ensuring a sustainable and social economic development.

For example, the Emiratization initiative was taken by UAE which involved a professional work force strategy. It mainly emphasize on the utilization of citizens into the workforce. This initiative was very helpful in aligning with the cultural values. It also contributes to the promotion of local talent and preservation of national identity in the business sector.

Another notable example of fusion of innovation and tradition in UAE is the development of Al Marmom Smart Majlis. This initiative was taken in Dubai which is a great blend of traditional concept with modern technology. This Majlis comprise a place where numerous community members can gather and discuss about their important matters. It also promotes the value of inclusivity, hospitality, and connection between the Emirates people. Moreover, this modern technology also enhances the traditional Majlis experience with modern tools and smart screens. It helps the visitors to engage in sharing ideas within their community. It also comprises a smart seating area where users can be Involved in virtual meetings or any other activity within the community.

Quantum Decision-Making Processes in UAE:

Quantum management policies have been established which have brought a dynamic shift in the decision-making processes. It may reflect the commitment of the UAE to adaptability and agility. It has decentralized the decision-making authority in the UAE. Rather than depending on the top-down directors, it is making deliberate efforts to empower the leadership levels. This allows for rapid response to challenges which helps in increasing the culture of initiatives at all the organizational levels. Furthermore, UAE also works on Quantum Management principles which help in empowering the collaborations between the private and public departments.

This approach can lead to an increase in innovation. It is done by blending the resources and the diverse expertise which creates a joint decision-making experience and helps in overcoming contemporary challenges. For example, the decision that was taken by UAE officials for the launch of the Emirates Mars Mission which was also known as Hope Probe exemplifies the agility of the UAE in utilizing big opportunities. Because this project was executed with rapid speed and in less time, it showcases the ability of the UAE to adapt to numerous space exploration techniques.

Another notable example of this includes the response of the UAE to covid-19 pandemic. At that time, the government implemented many rapid measures including vaccination camps, testing campaigns, lockdowns, which help in promoting public health. This was a proactive approach to this alarming situation. So, all these initiatives, projects, and programs tell about the UAE's commitment to agile decision-making. It ranges from crisis response, and utilizing opportunities to adapting to different global conditions. Hence, the UAE has been playing a major role as a dynamic player in the international economic landscape.

Quantum Social Architecture:

Quantum management also extends to the economic backgrounds in the UAE. It is the social architecture through numerous initiatives that are taken by the UAE for prioritizing diversity and community engagement. The first example of quantum social architecture includes the National Tolerance Program. This program demonstrates the use of quantum management principles in social architecture by aiming at a culture of acceptance and tolerance. It helps in embracing diversity. This initiative was taken by the UAE government to promote the connection between the religious and cultural communities. As a result, it leads to a harmonious and inclusive society.

Another example includes Inclusive Vision 2021. It was also an initiative that was started by the UAE which emphasized social inclusivity. This initiative works by setting its target for creating an inclusive and diverse society. The initiatives that were conducted under this Vision 2021 helped promote tolerance and inclusivity. They help in promoting an environment where people from different backgrounds are valued and accepted.

The third example in this regard includes cultural diplomacy in which the quantum management principles in UAE were adopted which was evident in the cultural diplomacy efforts. The notable event in this regard was Expo 2020 in Dubai which served as a big platform for cultural exchange around the globe. It helps in encouraging collaboration between diverse communities. Moreover, this approach also leads to an inclusive society that is based on both cultural and geographical boundaries.

All these initiatives helped in showcasing the principles of quantum management in UAE which as a result increased inclusivity, diversity, and collaboration in UAE society.

Quantum Work Culture:

Quantum management has shown a significant increase in the UAE Work Culture. It has increased the environment of innovation, employee empowerment, and flexibility. Numerous innovation-driven policies have been implemented by UAE which helps in promoting innovation among the workforce. In this regard, a notable initiative was taken named as National Innovation Strategy. The main aim of this initiative is to encourage businesses to invest in education and research. As a result, this will help in the promotion of a creative thinking culture and technological advancement. Moreover, these principles were also evident from the flexibility in the work organizations in UAE. They have many policies that support flexible hours and remote working which maintain a balance between the personal and professional life.

The main example of this Is hub71, which is a technology ecosystem. This initiative is based in Dubai which promotes the quantum work culture and provides a supportive environment for numerous technical companies and startups. It not only offers the physical working area but also remote working flexibility. So its main emphasis is on community engagement and innovative development through the use of quantum management principles.

Another notable example includes Strata Manufacturing which is an aerospace company based in Al Ain. It also works on the quantum work culture which promotes employee empowerment and commitment to work. This company promotes skill development, continuous learning, and international collaborations with a sustainable working environment.

Mubadla Investment Company is also an example of a quantum work culture. It is a wealth fund in Abu Dhabi that works on the quantum work culture. It mainly participates in the healthcare sector, renewable energy, and technical centers by demonstrating a forward-thinking approach. It also adapts to the different global economic changes through the expert approach which aligns with Quantum management principles. These examples depict how the different organizations in the UAE are working on the principles of quantum work culture which as a result promotes flexibility, employee empowerment, and innovation. This helps in navigating the complexities of different businesses.

Challenges in Implementing Quantum Management:

Numerous challenges are faced while adopting quantum management principles in different types of businesses. The first challenge in this regard is the cultural shift that is required while implementing the quantum management principles. This is because the traditional businesses work only on the traditional methods and resist moving on to the decentralized decision-making principles. Due to their resistance, it is a big challenge for different workplaces to align with the quantum management principles. Secondly, the employees can also be a big factor in resisting change through quantum management. So this is a big challenge for overcoming this resistance by employees and promoting a change in their work culture.

Thirdly, there are numerous data security concerns associated with Quantum management. This is because it uses data-driven decision-making through which organizations face fear related to their privacy and data. So building trust among the individuals of the organization regarding their data privacy is very crucial.

Adaptive Strategies and Lessons:

By considering all the above challenges regarding quantum management principles, there are numerous adaptive strategies for a successful future. The organizations can introduce gradual changes for a Quantum Management approach which will help face challenges. Secondly, effective communication will also be beneficial for transparency in decision-making processes. This will also help in making trustworthy employees during the journey of change which will help in addressing the resistance.

Furthermore, the organizations also invest in different leadership development programs for overcoming leadership challenges. These programs will help adapt the leadership skills which will empower the leaders to build a culture of innovation and guide the team members.

Moreover, to address data security concerns, organizations can work on cyber security measures. These include implementing encryption policies, usage of security technology, and ensuring compliance with the privacy regulations this training program can be conducted for employees on data security which will be very essential practice for them.

Overall, the Quantum Management exploration in UAE is a distinctive approach for social economic governance. It highlights the strategies of the UAE government for the integration of quantum management principles. It is involved in numerous departments which fosters innovation, adaptability, and forward-thinking in individuals. The application of Quantum Management in UAE from cultural fusion, decentralized decision-making, innovation ecosystem, social architecture, and adaptive economic strategies. So in the next chapter, we will be exploring different dimensions of Quantum Management in UAE. We will be discussing how Quantum management has become very important in the socio economic excellence of the UAE.

CHAPTER 5

QUANTUM FINANCE AND ECONOMIC PARADIGM

In case you don't know, Quantum finance plays a very important role in shaping the economy of the UAE. This is all because it utilizes quantum computing which is far more professional than the classical computational methods. This innovative approach is beneficial for the economic landscape of the UAE. Following are the aspects that contribute to the impact of Quantum Finance in UAE.

Quantum algorithms are used for solving numerous mathematical problems which help in more expert and sophisticated Quantum financial models in UAE. These models are used in terms of investment models, pricing models, and risk assessments.

Secondly, Quantum finance also plays a major role in mitigating the risk associated with cybersecurity. Moreover, Quantum cryptography helps in increasing the cybersecurity measures which ensures the protection of sensitive financial data.

These Quantum algorithms can also help in analyzing the big data sets which gives a major understanding of market dynamics. This ability of quantum algorithms helps in enhancing the decision-making processes. As a result, the Financial Institutions in UAE can respond to numerous shifts in the market trends ultimately leading to an adaptive and efficient economic environment. Adopting these Quantum Finance principles in the UAE helps in fostering the competitiveness in the global market. This increases investment in all these Quantum technologies. UAE is spreading its commitment to financial innovation and the attraction of international talents. Let's explore through this chapter.

Quantum Management Principles in Financial Modeling:

Quantum computing principles are fundamentally used for altering financial models. This is done by the power of superposition. It allows for assigning computation of different scenarios which provides a big advantage of quantum models over the classical computing financial methods. Superposition in portfolio optimization plays a very important role in Quantum algorithms. It facilitates diversified investment strategies which helps in enhancing the returns by considering different potential outcomes. Moreover, Quantum entanglement also helps in examining the financial variables. This is because financial modeling means gathering intricate data from diverse assets which leads to to accurate presentation of changing market trends.

Quantum Management Principles for Risk Analysis:

A major cornerstone of risk analysis is *Monty Carlo Simulations*, which were run with the help of numerous Quantum algorithms rather than the classical methods. They help accelerate the assessment of numerous risk scenarios which offers an understanding of financial downfalls. Secondly, *VaR modeling* also involves quantum computers which help in handling numerous complex calculations. This helps in processing the light data sets rapidly and enhances the precision of the potential losses that can occur due to the changing market conditions. This leads to more rapid risk management.

Future Directions:

Quantum computers make many noise and errors. So they can cause much damage to the financial models. This can be improved by developing error correction techniques which is very important for maintaining the integrity of the financial models that helps in analyzing different risk. Secondly, integrating the quantum algorithms with the traditional methods in the hybrid model can easily address the limitations and help in increasing the overall reliability of different financial applications.

So Quantum Finance helps in revolutionizing financial models and also overcomes the risk associated with quantum management principles. These Quantum algorithms help empower dictions. As these Quantum algorithms are making advancements they are redefining the financial landscape and offering more efficient insights into the quantum world.

Shaping an efficient Quantum-driven economic ecosystem:

There are numerous policies and strategies associated with the steps involved in shaping an efficient Quantum-driven economic landscape in the UAE. Following are the details of every policy along with its strategy for robust economic development.

Quantum Research and Development:

UAE has established numerous funding and incentives for Quantum research and development purposes. This policy was adopted to increase the economy of the UAE. For this, they use public-private partnerships and institutional collaborations. These collaborations help them in accelerating the advancements through Quantum technologies. This was very helpful in shaping the technology of the UAE.

Education and Workforce Development:

UAE also adopted a policy of implementing educational campaigns and programs that were normally based on Quantum technologies. These educational programs were implemented at different vocational centers, institutions, and universities. For this, UAE uses the strategy of a skilled Quantum workforce. This workforce was made expert in their field through different workshops, initiative campaigns, training sessions, and partnerships with quantum computing companies.

Public-Private Partnerships:

UAE has adopted a policy for facilitating the partnerships between the public and private sectors. This partnership was based on the quantum projects. For this, they started numerous initiatives that helped encourage different businesses to invest in quantum management applications. Here the business will focus on different industries including healthcare, finance, and logistics. This will help develop a great collaboration between public and private officials.

International Collaborations:

UAE has also actively participated in numerous International collaborations for the quantum principles. For this, they adopted the strategy of fostering the partnerships of organizations with countries at the international level. This helps in promoting the joint initiative and the knowledge exchange between the individuals of both countries. So, by implementing all these strategies and policies, the UAE laid the foundation for an efficient Quantum-driven ecosystem. This leads to a robust increase in their economy and innovation which also maintains sustainability in the time of quantum technologies.

Examples of Efficient Quantum Ecosystems:

Numerous examples tell you about the quantum-driven economic ecosystem of the UAE. This is because the UAE is proactively participating in many innovative technologies. Because of this, its economic landscape has also evolved. Following are some of the notable examples and initiatives that will tell you about the quantum-driven economic ecosystem of the UAE.

- **Collaboration with IBM**

These are the most notable examples of quantum computing collaborations. UAE collaborated with IBM which is a Global Technology leader. *IBM Quantum hub* was established in Abu Dhabi. It was done after a partnership with the innovation center in Abu Dhabi named *hub71*. The collaboration between both these technical leaders helped the UAE get more advancement in the quantum computing world. This led to an increase in the research and education in this region.

- **Research in Universities:**

Quantum finance was also involved in the research and development sectors in different universities. A University in UAE named *Khalifa University of Science and Technology* had invested in the Quantum research task. This was an initiative that helped the UAE build more talent and expertise in the quantum world.

- **Quantum Safe Blockchain:**

UAE has also integrated the quantum-safe blockchain cryptography networks. This was the main aim of the UAE to make its position stable in the field of blockchain technology. For this, the UAE incorporated numerous security measures related to Quantum resistance. So this has helped them enhance the reliability and trust of blockchain applications and numerous areas.

UAE as a Global Financial Powerhouse in Quantum Era:

UAE has made many efforts to become a financial hub globally in this Quantum age. For this, it has adopted numerous strategies and policies. *Firstly*, the main aim of the UAE was to position itself as a prime leader in the quantum finance world. For this, it has made many investments and the research in development sector and has implemented numerous Quantum Finance technologies. All these efforts have helped them build a financial ecosystem filled with talented people and cutting-edge technologies.

Secondly, the UAE also has an aim of enhancing the conducive environment for quantum innovations. For this, the UAE has developed many rules and regulations for using quantum technologies. This has ensured much clarity and security in its Quantum working. Moreover, it has also promoted Financial Solutions based on Quantum Technology.

Thirdly, the quantum computing infrastructure has also a main role in the success of the UAE. This is because the UAE wants to give a world-class Quantum education and resources to businesses all around the globe. For this purpose, it invested in numerous Quantum computing techniques which helped it make an international business. This has been done through International collaborations, partnerships, and the attraction of different Quantum ventures.

At last, UAE also wants to get experienced talent from all over the world in the field of quantum finance. For this, they implemented numerous initiatives to attract different Quantum scientists, developers, researchers, and professionals to create a skilled workforce.

With the help of all these strategies and efforts, the UAE has become a global power in the field of quantum finance. Furthermore, in this era of Quantum Technol, the UAE is fostering more International businesses, innovation, technology, and research and is helping to make the future of the people of UAE bright through the help of Quantum Finance.

Initiatives Attracting International Businesses:

UAE has started various initiatives to attract foreign Investments and other businesses from all over the globe. This collaboration has helped them in increasing economic growth and diversification. Following are some of the notable initiatives taken by UAE for Vision 2050:

- **Abu Dhabi Investment Office:**

This initiative was taken by the UAE to increase foreign investments. This entity has actively participated in promoting new investments from all around the world. It also helps in providing accurate information regarding the businesses. Moreover, it helps in determining the aim of businesses if they want to establish or expand it. This initiative in UAE is very helpful for a bright future for UAE businesses.

- **Foreign Direct Investment Laws:**

Foreign Direct Investment stands for FDI, which allows for promoting international collaborations and investments. The changes in these laws are made by the UAE for a strong commitment to an investment-friendly business ecosystem. As a result, this has helped in promoting international partnerships with the businesses in UAE.

- **Dubai Internet City:**

Dubai Internet City is considered a central point for innovation and technology. It is attracting many new technical companies, businesses, and startups for collaboration internationally. Due to this reason, many people are coming to the UAE for partnerships regarding tech projects. This is all because of the skilled workforce in Dubai Internet City and the professional technical tasks done here. This is done to become a part of the rising technological ecosystem by both parties. So this initiative will also be fruitful in the future UAE.

- **Expo 2020 Dubai:**

Dubai Expo 2020 is also abig initiative by the UAE for its commitment to becoming a global center for cultural exchange and business. This expo helped in attracting many foreign visitors and investors for business collaboration. This leads to increased economic growth and will also help the UAE in future businesses. So, by hosting this big event, has taken the initiative for its prosperous and bright future.

Challenges and Adaptive Strategies:

There are numerous challenges associated with the implementation of quantum finance principles. Following are the challenges and the adaptive strategies for all of them.

- **Integration with Traditional Systems:**

This is one of the biggest challenges of quantum financing, which involves the integration of quantum systems with traditional systems. This poses many challenges in the technical field. For this, businesses can easily develop numerous hybrid models comprising both quantum and traditional characteristics. They can also invest in the middleware which will help in increasing the interaction between the quantum and the traditional systems.

- **Security Concerns:**

Quantum computers possess many security concerns as compared to the recent cryptography methods. This is a big challenge in the quantum finance industry. So an adaptive strategy of investing in safe cryptographic methods and developing encryption standards can be a big effort for revolution. A secure Quantum communication system will help in collaborating with the International people without any security concerns.

Global Collaboration and Standardization:

Having less Quantum Technologies according to the Global standards is also a big challenge in this regard. This challenge can be alarming while investing in international businesses. For this, the businesses are actively participating in numerous foreign collaborations and contribute to the standardization techniques. This will help in the global economy based on the quantum Technology standards.

So, with the help of all the strategies for overcoming these challenges, Quantum finance can be a big economic key factor for the UAE. Numerous proactive strategies can be adopted by businesses to maximize their economy through the use of quantum technologies. It will also help in addressing all the recent complexities associated with Quantum Finance.

Reflection on Economic Transformation:

Quantum finance has played a very important role in shaping the economic landscape. It has a big potential for transforming the economy of any country. This will have a great impact on GDP growth, economic stability, and the employment of any sector.

Firstly, considering the GDP growth, Quantum Finance can increase this with its optimization of the financial processes. It will also help in making the decision-making process smooth. Here, quantum finance will play a major role in risk management and advanced modeling will help in higher GDP growth. As a result, technological activities will be stimulated and the need for investments will be attracted.

Secondly, Quantum finance also helps in catalyzing the innovation and the development of new industries. Numerous factors contribute to economic diversification which includes Quantum computing, Quantum applications, and Quantum cryptography. As a result, these innovations will help position the economy of the region globally and will make more advancements in the technology sector.

Thirdly, due to the Quantum Finance principles, *Global competitiveness* is also increasing. This is done by the attraction of foreign Investments. This will also help in increasing the quantum management workforce which will help in positioning the nation as number one in the quantum economic landscape. As a result, this will help attract multinational companies for economic stability.

Vision 2050: Economic Continuity:

Quantum finance is playing a major role in shaping the future of the UAE in 2050. It has a big and direct impact on the economic situation of the country. In this regard, Quantum finance plays a very major role in the economic diversification in the traditional sectors. It also helps in making more accurate financial strategies. For example, the use of quantum technologies contributes to diverse sectors with the help of numerous investment strategies. Moreover, Quantum computing also helps in their risk management enabling more economic growth.

In this regard, the quantum risk models are built for analyzing the potential economic threats. It helps in the economic resilience. Furthermore, vision 2050 of UAE is based on technology leadership. For this, quantum finance helps in making the UAE a global leader in the Financial Technology Sector. This is done through investments in the research and development sector of quantum computing which helps in increasing the position of UAE in the financial technology sector.:

Overall, the Quantum Finance plays a vital role in transforming the economic sector of the UAE. Many new initiatives have been taken that propelled the nation to become the number one country in the world in terms of innovation, technology, research, and development. The journey of UAE is comprised of commitment to the technology sector at a global scale. Now as we move on to the next chapters, we will be exploring how quantum management principles are important in the UAE journey. We will be getting all the details of the quantum management layers that will have a big impact on the position of the UAE as a center of progress and innovation.

CHAPTER 6

QUANTUM LEADERSHIP NAVIGATING THE FUTURE:

Quantum Leadership shows a big shift in the leadership roles in the UAE. It has taken inspiration and ideas from quantum mechanics. This is done to address all the complexities and challenges of the modern Quantum World. Quantum leadership helps in acknowledging the interconnectedness for overcoming different global challenges. So, in the context of the journey of UAE, the leadership approach helps in increasing change and embracing adaptability.

At the core of Vision 2050 of UAE, Quantum leadership is playing a central role by performing well over the traditional models. It mainly focuses on collaboration and investments internationally while acknowledging that they will be achieving success in the future through these techniques and strategies. This leadership design helps the leaders to act as a big motivation for creating risk-free environments where innovation is also embellished. Moreover, this Quantum Leadership recognizes the importance of the evolving landscape of quantum management.

So the big leaders in UAE are adaptable for all the changing situations regarding the quantum leaderships. Furthermore, it also plays a major role in fostering a culture of learning and adaptation. It helps encourage new ideas, innovation, technology, and global trends which ensures that the UAE will become a big innovation center in the future. With the help of this approach, the UAE can actively participate in shaping its destiny in the future.

Essence of Quantum Leadership:

- **Adaptability:**

The essence of quantum leadership from the base of quantum leadership adaptability is the main principle. Here leaders operate within the adaptive framework that helps in overcoming the changing situations. The leaders help in embracing uncertain changes which help them in growing rather than becoming hindrances for them. A Quantum Leader is always capable of adopting professional strategies in response to the changing economic conditions. This adaptability feature in the quantum leaders enables them to navigate with confidence among different territories.

For example, a Quantum leader in UAE, *Her Excellency Reem Al Hashmey* was the UAE minister of state for international collaboration. She was also the director general of Expo 2020 Dubai, who has shown outstanding and professional adaptability in leadership. As an important leader in UAE, her ambition for a successful future is demonstrated by her adaptive strategies for ensuring the success of numerous initiatives of which Expo 2020 Dubai was also one of them. Her leadership qualities have increased the importance of flexibility in responding to numerous complex global challenges.

- **Fostering Innovation:**

Innovation is a basic tool of quantum leadership. So the leaders who are under this Quantum leadership create an environment of innovation and creativity. They adopt every strategy for overcoming the risks associated with technology and innovation. So by adopting a culture of innovation, Quantum Leadership can easily excel in their organizations for progress. Moreover, considering the journey of UAE the commitment of quantum leaders for innovation and technology becomes a very important tool for gaining ambitious goals. This helps in ensuring that the nation will always be at the front considering advancements in numerous sectors.

For example, Mohammed Alabbar who is the founder of Emma Properties is known for outstanding projects including Burj Khalifa, which shows a big innovative commitment to the country. Under his leadership, Dubai has increased its prosperity and reputation among different cities of the UAE. This was all because of his focus on different groundbreaking ventures and projects. One of the main projects was "Dubai Mall of the World" which highlighted his dedication to innovation and technology through the use of quantum leadership principles.

- **Visionary Thinking:**

Quantum leadership also plays a major role in visionary thinking. This is because the leaders are intended towards the encouragement of transcending the classical boundaries. This helps in increasing the possibilities that will give slow but beneficial results. So by adopting a forward-looking approach, quantum leaders can easily inspire the world in terms of innovation and technology. This visionary thinking and approach can lead to the fulfillment of UAE'UAE'tUAE's 2050.

For example, *His Highness Sheikh Mohammed bin Rashid Al Maktoum* who is the prime minister and also the vice president of UAE is considered a big ruler of Dubai. He is a visionary leader. Sheikh Mohammed has a great forward-thinking approach to UAE. This is evident from his numerous initiatives including the Mars Science City project. He has a great commitment to a prosperous future of the UAE for which he has made many innovations through his Quantum leadership abilities.

Hence, the essence of quantum leadership mainly relies on visionary thinking, adaptability, and innovation power. These are the main principles that will help navigate the complexities for a better future in the UAE.

Leadership in Times of Change:

Quantum leadership has played a very important role in transforming the future of the UAE through its dynamic decisions and adaptability to numerous changing situations. One of the most illustrated examples is the response of the UAE to the decline in prices of oil in 2014. At that time, the UAE leader's main aim was diversification in their economic sectors including tourism, renewable energy, and technology instead of relying on oil resources. This strategy has helped them make adaptive and proactive decisions for safeguarding the nation's impact in the changing oil market.

Secondly, the response of these Quantum leaders to COVID-19 is also one major example of quantum leadership. At that time, the leaders took swift action to protect the health of the public. This was all done to manage the crisis. So at that time, the quantum leadership principles were evident from different initiatives including the "10 Million Meals campaign". This campaign was run to provide food and address the needs of the suffering community. This was done to prioritize both the public health as well as the social well-being of the people in this crisis period.

So quantum leadership is always a guiding force in the UAE journey for Vision 2050. This is all because of its transformative actions which emphasize dynamic decision-making and crisis management with forward-thinking abilities.

Quantum-Inspired Decision-Making:

Quantum leadership has used tum-inspired decision-making principles which mainly emphasize the use of data. The big leaders in UAE have used numerous technologies and advanced analytics for gathering data and getting a deep understanding of numerous complex situations. This approach has helped them in making informed decisions which ensures an empirical approach for innovation. So by the use of data power, leaders can easily navigate difficult situations with accuracy and precision. This will align with the quantum principles for accurate and clear decision-making processes.

Moreover, quantum leadership also encourages the ers to adopt uncertainty in different steps of decision-making. Because of this, UAE leaders have acknowledged the changing environment which allows for an adaptable decision-making process. Hence, by accepting the uncertainty, leaders can easily apply innovative solutions that are available for all unexpected opportunities. All these things will be aligned with the quantum principles to adhere to unpredictable situations.

One more primary element of quantum leadership is decentralized decision-making processes. In this, the leaders help encourage the teams and make them prepare for making autonomous decisions. This helps in creating a culture of agility and innovation. So this decentralized approach helps in making quick and accurate responses for the changing situations. It also helps in promoting accountability and ownership among the different team members. Considering the UAE, this decentralized Quantum decision-making is highly evident from numerous initiatives that help in empowering the innovative sectors. This also contributes to the adaptability and overall resilience of the nation.

Quantum-inspired decision-making has numerous notable examples. The first example includes UAE AI Strategy 2031. This uses data-driven insights for a better future for the UAE. It helps in making a comprehensive data analysis for the development of AI. This decision helps in making precise and informed decisions that align with the quantum principles.

Other examples of the decision-making processes with the help of quantum management principles include *Dubai International Financial Centre* and *Abu Dhabi Global Market*. Both these projects are the free zones that have been inspired by the quantum principles. These are the best approaches for decentralized decision-making. All these free zones help operate autonomously and will empower the policies that will foster international business and innovation. So the decision to create these types of free zones is a big commitment to the decentralization processes in UAE which allows for an increase in economic conditions and diversification of the UAE.

These real-life examples help show the influence of quantum leadership in the d how it has made impactful decisions. These decisions are made by embracing uncertainty and leveraging data-driven insights. As a result, it has encouraged the decision-making processes for driving progress and innovation.

Shaping Organizational Culture:

There are numerous strategies for shaping the organizational cultures in the UAE. These include fostering innovation, encouraging collaboration, empowering employees, etc. Following are the details and examples of all these principles required for shaping the organizational cultures in UAE.

Fostering Innovation:

The quantum leadership principles are used for shaping the culture of the UAE with the help of numerous innovative commitments. The leaders in UAE implement numerous strategies and policies for encouraging improvement and creativity in cultural settings. Numerous initiatives have been taken including the research ground center programs and innovation house which will help in empowering the organizational growth. This strategy emphasizes innovative techniques that align with leadership skills. Here the leaders recognise the importance of exploring new possibilities for staying ahead in the changing modern world.

A notable example of fostering innovation in cultural settings includes *Emirates Airlines*. It has used numerous Quantum leadership strategies for increasing innovation in the aircraft industry. This company has invested in numerous technologies for developing an advanced flight mechanism and to enhance the comfortable passenger experience. Additionally, one more example includes Emirates Aviation X lab, which is a big commitment to innovative solutions that align with the quantum leadership principles.

Empowering Employees:

The quantum leadership principles have also helped in empowering the employees in numerous settings which promotes a sense of ownership. Numerous policies have been adopted for flexible work engagement, mentorship programs, training campaigns, and skill development initiatives. All these initiatives are taken to empower individuals for their professional and personal growth. This approach always goes well with the quantum management principles for adaptability. Here the employees are encouraged to navigate the changing circumstances of the business world.

A notable example of this includes *Chalhoub Group*, which is a leading retailer in luxury. It is based in the Middle East and it uses numerous Quantum leadership principles that have empowered its employees and workforce. The main aim of this company is to focus on employee development which is done through training sessions and mentorship programs. The Chalhoub Group aligns with the principles of quantum leadership which fosters the sense of ownership among all the employees.

Encouraging Collaboration:

Different organizations in the UAE are influenced by the quantum leadership principles in which the leaders have promoted these functional channels facilitate the exchange of ideas. Many initiatives are also taken to bring together all the perspectives from diverse backgrounds which reflect the interconnectedness in the business environment. As a result, it increases the collaborative environment and creates a dynamic space for innovation and collective intelligence. For example, *Dubai Investment Company* is a strategic company in the UAE that uses Quantum leadership values for collaboration. It has also partnerships with numerous companies around the world which has helped it in addressing the complex challenges. This strategic investment company reflects the collaborative nature of the business landscape that emphasizes success through collaboration.

Quantum Leadership in Government:

The quantum leadership principles are applied by the numerous government sectors which help in the promotion of agility. The UAE government has also implemented numerous initiatives notably the smart government program. This program has helped them increase the technologies and streamline the processes. This emphasizes ensuring that the government organizations can easily adapt to the evolving circumstances.

The quantum leadership in government is also reflected through an initiative like the "*Happiness Agenda*". This initiative mainly prioritizes the satisfaction of citizens and their well-being. It also has a big commitment to citizen-centric approach. With the help of this, the government of UAE can easily exemplify the responsive mindset which ensures alignment with the evolving circumstances.

As a result, quantum leadership is applied in numerous government sectors which is evident through their policies and strategies for responsiveness, adaptability, and decision-making. All these initiatives collectively make the UAE government dynamic and highly evolving for all the needs of citizens.

Quantum Leadership and Global Influence:

The quantum leadership principles also contribute to influencing the UAE on the global level. The leaders adopt agile strategies and forward-thinking approaches for evolving in numerous International diplomatic initiatives. One of the most motivational examples of this is the *Dubai Expo 2020*, which showcases the global collaboration of the UAE. In this initiative, the quantum leaders have strengthened diplomatic relationships and economic partnerships with other countries. This helps the UAE to become a major player in shaping the future of the UAE. Secondly, Quantum Leadership also helps in active collaborations internationally. So UAE has now become a bridge between different regions to foster stability and encourage rapid progress on a global stage. Numerous UAE leaders have initiated international collaborations. For example, *Sheikh Fatima Binte Mubarak who was* the chairwomen of the General Women's Union is a big visionary leader of the UAE. She has played a vital role in making advancements in women's rights. She has started initiatives like the "*Mother of the Nation festival*" which contributes to gender equality and encourages family values. Her visionary leadership has made UAE a champion for women's empowerment internationally.

Another notable leader of the UAE is *Mohammed Bin Zayed Al Nahyan* who is the Crown Prince of Abu Dhabi. He has shown his strategic leadership skills globally through numerous initiatives. His notable initiative includes *Mars Shot*, which shows commitment to space exploration. By addressing the global issues regarding space research, Mohammad Bin Zayed has actively participated in exploring new perspectives for space exploration.

Vision 2050: A Continuation:

The quantum leadership principles are useful in making the framework of sustained leadership in the UAE. It is done by fostering visionary leadership, and adaptability, empowering future leaders, and promoting innovation. All these principles create a very prominent and big foundation for advancement in the nation.

Firstly, the quantum leadership principles also lay the foundation for the vision 2050 excellence by focusing mainly on adaptability. The leaders adopting the quantum principles in this evolving world help in navigating unforeseen changes and circumstances. This ability has helped with ensuring effectiveness and is very crucial for gaining long-term goals.

Moreover, visionary leadership is also playing a main role in the successful vision 2050 of UAE. So by embracing the forward-thinking approach and strategies for the ambitious goals, the leaders have been creating a thorough road map for the progress of the UAE. They have a big ability to foster a sense of right direction which ensures the achievement of long-term objectives.

Furthermore, Quantum leadership values are also involved in the empowerment of future leaders. This is because the vision of 2050 can easily be accelerated with the help of the empowerment of the upcoming generation with their mindset and skills. For this educational initiative training campaigns, mentorship programs, arms, and other opportunities were created that contribute to the betterment of the nation with the values of quantum leadership.

Conclusion:

In this chapter, we have discussed the quantum leadership role in transforming UAE's ambitious journey. It has played an important role in realizing the vision of 2050. This is because quantum leadership principles have emerged as a key factor for shaping the nation's future with the help of visionary thinking, innovation, adaptability, and commitment to excellence. As we move on to the next chapter, we will be exploring the further aspects of quantum management in the journey of UAE. We will be discussing how Quantum management principles will be a driving force in propelling the nation's future.

CHAPTER 7

EDUCATING THE QUANTUM GENERATION

In this rapidly growing world of technology, the UAE is also making advancements in the Quantum Sciences. In this Quantum era, the UAE is playing a main role in educating the people regarding this. This is because Quantum Sciences and Quantum technology are playing a very important role in revolutionizing problem-solving strategies and communication which is very helpful for the upcoming generation. This is because education plays a very important role in this transformative world. So involving quantum tools and technology in the new generation of education can easily increase the learning experience. For example, Quantum computing is very helpful in providing computation capabilities to individuals. This helps in enabling the students to solve complex simulations and scenarios.

Quantum Technology in Learning:

There are numerous technologies associated with quantum management principles that can be integrated into learning for a prosperous future. Firstly, virtual *labs* can be created through quantum technology which can increase the learning processes. It also helps in simulating the complex quantum situations. In this way, students can easily interact with numerous Quantum systems. This will be helpful for them to get hands-on experience in the digital environment, which can also help them to change the circumstances. This professional approach by UAE will help in encouraging understanding and experimentation without physical contact.

Secondly, the students will also be provided with access to *Quantum computing sources*. It is a game changer in this modern world because the Quantum computing platforms are very helpful for learners to solve quantum calculations. This will also give them a unique experience of using Quantum machines to get an understanding of the computational power. This direct access to quantum computing will help the students in fostering a sense of understanding of the computing principles. It will also prepare students for the changing technology world.

Thirdly, the students can also get a more in-depth knowledge of quantum computing with the help of quantum information, processing modules. By integrating these modules into the curriculum, the students can easily get an in-depth knowledge of algorithms and cryptography. These interactive modules are very helpful for a student in learning the principles of quantum information theory. Moreover, they will also get engaged in quantum communication and this exposure will help them lay the foundation for future Quantum computing innovations.

Lastly, the students can also understand quantum technologies with the help of exploring quantum Communication protocols. This will help them in understanding the integration of quantum technologies. This exposure will be a well-developed education exposure for all the students in the field of quantum information science. This is because they will get key insights into the potential usage of secure communication. So, by incorporating all the elements and strategies into the learning processes the students will be helped with Quantum powered future. This is because quantum technologies will give them a long pathway for an engaging and dynamic educational experience. It will also help them in preparing for different opportunities and challenges coming in the future.

There are numerous examples of education institutions in the UAE that work on the centric approach. The students can easily a get hands-on learning experience in these institutions. This is because the UAE has invested in Quantum technologies in the educational field because of the changing Quantum era. So following are some of the key initiatives taken by UAE keeping in view the quantum education.

1. One of the key initiatives taken was the *UAE National Quantum program*. The main aim of this program is to prepare a skilled future workforce. This is a government-driven initiative that supports quantum education through the use of quantum technology. It represents the UAE government's approach to fostering technology and innovation for future students.
2. Moreover, this *STEM Quantum education* is also a main Education Centre in UAE. It stands for Science, Technology, Engineering, and Mathematics where students are encouraged to participate in the engineering, technology, science, and mathematics field and become future leaders. This advanced stem education comprises of advanced curriculum for the students to get exposure to professional Quantum principles.
3. Furthermore, the UAE has also developed many universities and research centers that work on Quantum principles. UAE has also collaborated with International partnerships to gain expertise in quantum education Institutions. Numerous joint programs have been started that focus on quantum technologies. All these developments in the quantum education are dynamic. They provide you with the most accurate and professional knowledge regarding quantum Technology.

Quantum Skills Development:

There are numerous strategies adopted for developing quantum skills in the students. Following are the strategies adopted by different educational institutions and organizations in UAE.

Structured Courses:

This strategy includes implementing professional and expert quantum courses in the curriculum of universities or colleges. It covers different Quantum computing principles, Quantum Mechanics, and Quantum science studies. This will help in incorporating hands-on experience in the real-world applications and the virtual labs which will provide the students with a great practical Quantum experience. Moreover, these courses will add a new strength to the education field for future purposes.

Online Learning Platforms:

This initiative is also very helpful for promoting quantum education in the students. There will be new courses of Quantum tutorials and interactive modules on different platforms. These platforms may include *Microsoft, Quantum development kit, IBM Quantum experience*, etc which will be offering the resources to the students. These resources will be helpful for both the beginners as well as for the advanced children which will foster a good space of learning.

Quantum Certification:

Many certificate programs also started in UAE which will contribute to the promotion of quantum education among the students. The certificate programs are started in collaboration with different Quantum learning platforms. The sources of the certification programs include *IBM, Microsoft,* and other validated Quantum programs. These programs will be helpful for the professionals as well as for the beginner students to emerge in the skilled Quantum workforce.

Interdisciplinary Programs:

Many professional interdisciplinary programs are also developed for combining with the quantum concepts. These programs will be helpful in excellent in different fields including chemistry, science, computer, and engineering. Moreover, quantum technologies also offer intersection with numerous disciplines and these prepare individuals for numerous world-class applications.

So, by implementing all these strategies and initiatives, the education institutions in the UAE can easily contribute to the professional development of quantum education. The programs will help ensure the al-prepared and professional workforce in this Quantum era.

Quantum Ready Teachers:

There are numerous initiatives taken by UAE for the quantum-ready teachers. These teachers will specialize in different Quantum technologies to guide the students for the future success of UAEhe

Professional Workshops:

UAE has started conducting professional development workshops for teachers. These workshops and seminars will help make a good focus on the quantum-centric approach. Moreover, the sessions will cover teaching strategies, Quantum concepts, Quantum education, and the integration of all these Quantum technologies in numerous educational subjects. So these ongoing workshops and development seminars will be a big opportunity for ensuring that teachers will remain updated with all the latest Quantum Technology advancements. If they remain updated, they will be guiding the students in a more efficient manner which will be helpful for the upcoming generation.

Collaboration with Researchers:

UAE is also facilitating a good collaboration and partnership between the quantum researchers and the teachers in the education Institutions of UAE. This collaboration will help the educators get a deep insight into the current Quantum research, emerging technologies, and quantum applications. This will help in getting a better understanding of the quantum concepts for all the students.

Online Quantum Resources:

Numerous online platforms and resources are also developed by UAE for dedicated teachers to learn quantum education. These platforms will include Quantum lessons, interactive simulations, and the content that goes with the quantum educational standards. So this will be helpful for the teachers to incorporate the quantum educational topics in the classrooms and guide students regarding these topics.

Teacher Certification Programs:

UAE has also started many teacher certification programs that will include the quantum educational components. The programs will ensure that the teachers get all the information related to the quantum concepts which will prepare them to integrate the quantum education into the teaching practices. This will also help them in becoming a certified professional in the Quantum Technology field.

Lab Experience:

The teachers of UAE will also get hands-on experience in the labs regarding quantum research through these virtual labs. They will get practical exposure to all the quantum principles which will enhance their ability to convey practically about the quantum education. This will be a more engaging and professional educational method for all the students. For example, numerous teachers in the UAE have incorporated quantum concepts in their educational institutions. Following are the details of all those teachers and their approach to promoting quantum education in education institutions.

Dr Al Mansoori:

Dr Al Mansoori is a physics professor who teaches at UAE University. He integrates and uses numerous quantum mechanics in his lectures. This is done by him through numerous real-world examples and quantum demonstrations. He helps his students in grabbing all the related knowledge of the tum Tumcepts. Moreover, the teaching methods of Doctor Al Mansuri are innovative and unique which helps in fostering an environment of critical thinking. This will help the students in exploring the quantum sciences. Hence, the teaching methods of Doctor Al Mansoori are famous in UAE regarding quantum physics.

Mr Ahmed:

Mr Ahmed is a technology specialist in a UAE school. He has also integrated numerous Quantum computing procedures into the curriculum of computer science. Through his outstanding knowledge of quantum Technology, he guided the students regarding programming and quantum algorithms. This also helps the students by encouraging them to explore the new Quantum applications. This is all because of the forward-thinking approach of Mr Ahmed which aligns with the commitment of UAE to a prosperous and technical country in the world.

Dr Al Farsi:

Dr Al Farisi is a great educator of mathematics in UAE. He has incorporated numerous Quantum algorithms in the Math courses of his Institution through different coding exercises and hands-on experience on the collaborative quantum project. He has introduced the students to quantum computing. This is done by providing them with mathematical foundations. Moreover, the teaching methods of Doctor Al Farsi have built a big connection between Quantum technology and mathematics. This has helped the students in preparing for the numerous interdisciplinary changes.

Mr Abdullah:

Mr Abdullah is the coordinator of STEM education at a high school in the UAE. He helps in organizing different extracurricular activities including quantum education. Through his organized workshops and science clubs, he shows numerous Quantum concepts to the students which helps them in encouraging them to explore the Quantum Field. This initiative taken by him is also a big change for students in this Quantum era.

Quantum Education for Global Competitiveness:

Quantum education is very helpful to stand in the Global world of UAE because qum-centric education involves cutting-edge technical programs through which the country can easily become a professional destination for international students as well. They can come and seek higher education in quantum technology and science. This will bring a big professional talent to the UAE which will help create a skilled workforce. As a result, it will enhance the Global competitiveness of the UAE in the Quantum Field.

Moreover, quantum education will also help in collaborating with numerous International institutions. UAE can have joint research projects and academic partnerships with foreign Institutions which will help in acknowledging the dynamic Global network. These collaborations will help amplify the quantum research impact which will help UAE become a key player in the quantum community internationally. This Quantum education also helps in cultivating the culture of research and development. This is done by the UAE institutions that engage its students in quantum research and reinforce them to become leaders in the advancement of Quantum science.

In summary, quantum education will prepare the nation for standing globally. This will be done by attracting the first foreign talent and encouraging collaborations in making the country a key factor in the evolving field of quantum Technology.

Challenges and Adaptive Education:

There are numerous challenges associated with the quantum education initiative in the UAE. For them, many adaptive strategies are also taken. First, we will be talking about the challenges and then the adaptations for those challenges.

Rapid Technological Changes:

In this rapidly changing era of quantum technology, there are challenges associated with the rapid technology. It is a bit challenge nowadays to keep the educational curriculum of quantum education up to date. So for this, the Quantum curriculum of different Institutions must include and adhere to the latest advancements with the help of responsive educational strategies.

Limited Quantum Education Faculty:

The shortage of quantum-ready faculty is also a big challenge in quantum education. This is because it can cause disturbance in the effective and professional delivery of quantum education to the students. Through this, the institutions can face a big challenge in recruiting qualified instructors for quantum education. So to overcome this challenge, the institutions should conduct Quantum Central programs and search for qualified teachers to meet the Quantum education criteria.

Accessibility and Inclusivity:

These different initiatives of quantum education also suffer from accessibility issues. So they must address them to ensure that students from different backgrounds can easily have the opportunity to engage in these types of educational programs. This can be easily done with the help of overcoming the potential barriers. For this, they should design advanced mathematical knowledge that should be accessible to students from all backgrounds and educational levels.

Teacher Training:

In this Quantum educational world, teachers can face numerous challenges in acquiring quantum skills. This will be a big challenge to teach the quantum concepts to the student effectively. For this, continuous professional development programs are necessary for teachers and educators. This will help them to get a well equipped knowledge of delivering the quantum education to the students easily.

Overall, we have discussed the transformative effect of quantum education in the journey of UAE. This will help you to become a global competitor in achieving technological excellence. In this regard, UAE has a great strategic vision for quantum education which will be a cornerstone for economic diversification and societal advancement. As we move on to the next chapters, we will be discussing the strategic implementation of UAE for quantum technology. It will also show how the different policies will help shape the quantum landscape and will analyze the quantum industry collaborations.

CHAPTER 8

QUANTUM TECHNOLOGY IN THE UAE: A LEAP INTO THE FUTURE

Have you heard of the incredible leap into the future UAE is making? An area with incredible potential, quantum technology is being pioneered by one of the most advanced nations on earth--the United Arab Emirates (UAE). So what exactly is quantum technology? Simply put, it utilizes the remarkable physics of tiny atoms and particles to create powerful innovations. We're talking about new kinds of lightning-fast computing, unhackable communication, and ultra-precise sensors among other wonders! By tapping into the quantum realm, humanity can tackle challenges too difficult for regular technology. As a global innovation leader, the UAE is pumping massive investments so quantum breakthroughs catalyze all parts of society. Vision 2021 and Vision 2071 national development plans place technology and knowledge creation at the core. Quantum perfectly aligns with these goals. It will permit giant leaps in sectors like healthcare, transportation, energy and much more over the coming decades! Economic diversification is also a priority for the UAE as it transitions from an oil-dependent economy. Quantum opens exciting new industries centered around computing, software, photonics, cryptology and advanced materials. Rapid growth is expected - both for quantum export revenues and domestic consumption. This means a rising quality of life based on tech-powered productivity.

So in this chapter, we'll learn exactly how the UAE governments and companies are racing to deploy quantum solutions today to redefine tomorrow! Topics span computing, communications, AI, cybersecurity - unveiling how quantum technology permits the UAE to stretch possibilities to boundaries yet unimagined! Ready to dive in? Then let's explore together this unconditional future forged by the light of quantum innovation!

Advancing Quantum Computing

Do you know that the UAE is making significant strides in quantum computing research and development? A major initiative is the Quantum Research Center (QRC) under the Abu Dhabi Technology Innovation Institute. With renowned global experts like Executive Director Dr. Andrew Lütken, QRC aims to develop high-quality quantum processors. Current efforts focus on superconducting qubit architectures with plans to have 30+ qubits operational within two years. The priority is building resilient, practical systems rather than just racing for qubit counts.

Beyond hardware, QRC is training specialized talent and honing original algorithms to demonstrate quantum advantages. Multidisciplinary collaboration and international partnerships drive rapid progress. In education, NYU Abu Dhabi is fostering quantum interest through hackathons jointly organized with MIT and CERN. Attracting 150+ students, these boost computational skills while raising quantum computing visibility across industries. Overall, Abu Dhabi's methodical approach centers long-term economic dividends enabled by homegrown quantum technologies. With steady advancements in materials engineering, software libraries and skill development, the integrated strategy can position UAE as a leader guiding global computing evolution.

Quantum Computing as A Catalyst for Innovation

Quantum computing is one of the most promising and transformative quantum technology applications. Traditional computers encode information in the binary digits or "bits" 0s and 1s.

On the other hand, it uses quantum bits (or qubits) that employ unique properties of nature at a subatomic level. It may include superposition combined with those called entanglement to complete mathematical calculations. Through this process, quantum computers can overcome the limitations that even today's fastest supercomputers face. More specifically, quantum computing will help to improve the machine learning and artificial intelligence (AI) algorithms for complicated optimizations, predictions and analysis Applications include everything from drug discovery, clinical diagnostics to financial risk modeling and supply chain optimization. The UAE is investing heavily in quantum computing education, research and development.

Established in 2019, the Mohamed Bin Zayed University of Artificial Intelligence (MBZUAI) is based in Abu Dhabi and thus far represents the world's only graduate research university dedicated entirely to AI. At the same time as training new AI and quantum specialists, MBZUAI will research its application to variable quality data. The UAE also contains dedicated laboratories for quantum information within international branches of other universities, including University Of Science and Technology of China.

In addition, there are homegrown quantum computing startups like Qubit Systems. Qubit Systems, an architect of quantum processors using photonics, has teamed up with major UAE companies to explore applications for the technology. The UAE is also working with technology giants such as IBM to identify local applications for quantum computing, in both the private and public sectors.

Applications of Quantum in Various Sectors

Now we will be looking at the drastic applications of Quantum in various sectors. Quantum technology isn't just about computers—it's a game-changer across various fields, and the UAE is taking the lead in this quantum revolution. In finance, quantum computing is shaking up portfolio optimization, considering millions more risk variables than traditional systems. This allows financial institutions to navigate unexpected events better. Quantum Investing, a startup, is bringing these cutting-edge services to the market.

The asset management industry is also getting a quantum boost, using advanced algorithms for trading indicators and analysis. This translates to more sophisticated risk management and decision-making. Logistics giants like FedEx are exploring quantum computing to optimize delivery routes based on dynamic factors, benefiting companies like Emirates Logistics in the UAE, which can cut costs and reduce environmental impact. In e-commerce, quantum machine learning is a game-changer for forecasting inventory demand across a vast range of products, minimizing overstock and understock situations, and optimizing supply chain efficiency.

The oil and gas sector is tapping into quantum sensing and modeling tools for discovering new fields and reservoirs. Quantum physics is influencing materials development, with innovations like quantum dots having applications in solar panels. Cleantech startups like Quantum PowerPods are leveraging the UAE's solar infrastructure for sustainable energy solutions.

Healthcare is undergoing a quantum transformation, from accelerating pharmaceutical R&D to improving medical imaging and DNA sequencing. UAE-based providers like Biogenex Labs are at the forefront, offering these quantum-powered solutions locally. Wealthy individuals are willing to pay premiums for quantum genetic mapping, creating new opportunities in personalized healthcare. In communications, quantum physics ensures perfectly secure information encoding in quantum states, making message interception impossible without data destruction. The UAE is investing heavily in quantum communication infrastructure, including networks resistant to cyber-attacks. These initiatives will be crucial for aerospace, autonomous transport, and smart city initiatives where data security is paramount.

The UAE's proactive stance makes it a key player in shaping the quantum landscape across these diverse industries. From finance to healthcare, logistics to communications, quantum technology is unlocking new possibilities, and the UAE is at the forefront of this transformative wave.

Quantum Infrastructure Development
Building a Quantum Future

Let's now take a look at quantum infrastructure development that builds a quantum future. Technology leadership requires infrastructure spanning research, education, entrepreneurship and commercialization. Recognizing this, the UAE is constructing world-class quantum hubs enabling breakthroughs from lab to market!

The Emirates Research and Development Council founded the National Quantum Center where an all-star technology team pursues industry-defining innovations. State-of-the-art quantum computing labs, communication networks, sensor systems and nanotech facilities provide platforms to reimagine what's possible. International collaborations also connect researchers with elite global institutes.

Satellite Quantum Research Labs across Dubai develop specialized technologies - be it AI, simulation software or quantum cryptography. Training programs offered at these centers build coveted skill sets for students before joining either academia or corporate R&D. Intensive summer camps introduce quantum principles to young citizens, catalyzing tomorrow's inventors.

Hartmann Quantum Investments Fund provides grants to bubble-up commercially viable ideas through startup incubator challenges. Entrepreneurial ventures crafting quantum devices for health diagnostics or solar energy get physical resources like testing sandboxes alongside advisory mentors.

Patented technologies already emerging span satellite-based quantum communication, secure mobile networks, novel drug discovery algorithms and precision agriculture sensors. By 2025, over 50 homegrown quantum companies could uplift GDP while making technologies affordable to society.

Overall, spending on quantum infrastructure exceeds $400 million over the decade as part of the National Innovation Strategy. With fundamental research already demonstrating quantum advantages, the next step is bringing these learnings to life through entrepreneurial products benefiting all citizens. An enabling ecosystem integrating research, academia and business is helping accelerate this science to market journey - catapulting the UAE to pole position in next-gen tech like quantum!

Communication and Cybersecurity

While quantum enables disruptive civilian technologies, enhanced communication security is yet another key application. As digital infrastructure expands to power smart cities, IoT networks and autonomous mobility, corresponding vulnerabilities also grow. Quantum communication promises perfectly secured public and defense data channels resistant to emerging cyber threats.

By encoding signals in quantum states of photons, any attempt to eavesdrop immediately destroys the information - thus guaranteeing failsafe encryption. Such quantum key distribution (QKD) techniques can protect critical infrastructure. Further authentication methods like quantum fingerprinting prevent fake identity attacks. Quantum blockchain implementations also help share verifiable data between multiple parties without compromising privacy.

Accordingly, the UAE R&D Council has initiated efforts to build a national quantum communication backbone spanning government, defense agencies and critical industries. Terrestrial and satellite infrastructure developments are underway in partnership with global collaborators like the European Telecommunications Standards Institute. The Space Agency also runs a quantum encryption experiment aboard the UAE's Hope Mars spacecraft. Indeed, quantum-secured communications will be integral for protecting citizens' interests and rights as digital services expand. As an early testbed, Dubai Internet City is already piloting QKD to safeguard resident company data. Going forward, the quantuminfrastructure being deployed will be a bedrock for the UAE's technological transformation.

Acceleration of Economic Growth

By catalyzing new industries and optimizing traditional ones, quantum technology adoption steers the UAE's economic expansion. Recognizing vast potential, the National Quantum Strategy 2040 approved $6 billion in development funding - with over $350 billion returns expected! Specialized zones have already cultivated over 40 quantum ventures. Dubai Science Park packs infrastructure for startups to scale innovations from R&D to exports. On-site labs, computing resources and testing environments facilitate market-ready products.

One graduate - Optimized Robotics - sells machine learning solutions globally. Others actively working on breakthroughs span drug discovery, logistics, secure networks, sensors and much more. Indeed, diversifying beyond hydrocarbons into knowledge economy sectors centering quantum fits National Innovation Strategy directives. Extensive funds also sponsor domestic integration to elevate competitiveness. Private consultation houses help organizations transit to quantum computing for enhanced operations. Cloud service providers are integrating quantum algorithms within existing frameworks to adoption. And the public sector aims to demonstrate quantum capabilities via flagship initiatives around blockchain, AI and smart communities.

To stimulate more ideas, Technology Transfer Offices connect researchers with enterprises needing cutting-edge IP - be it around advanced materials, cryptography or imaging. Streamlined patent filing and licensing regulations incentivize commercialization. Such structures nourish the quantum ecosystem.

Workforce development programs likewise breed specialized talent, addressing expected quantum industry talent shortages locally. Academic degrees centering business applications teach requisite concepts while positioning graduates to drive adoption. And vocational training helps professionals from other domains cross-skill.

Cumulatively, these interlocked efforts to ease technology development, adoption barriers and skills availability expedite quantum's economic influence. Within a decade, a thriving community of enterprises reimagining everything from finance to agriculture to telecommunications could position the UAE as a quantum economic leader guiding international progression trajectories too!

Quantum Research and Development

The UAE recognizes that economic potential can only be realized through continued, extensive R&D in quantum science and technologies. This understanding has brought about wide-ranging investments into institutional research programs. The Quantum Research Center conducts studies into quantum computing algorithms, smart materials, quantum sensing principles and communication protocols to advance applications. Researcher talent is hired from across the world and collaborations have been established with leading universities in the USA, UK and China. Big breakthroughs generated domestically include patented techniques for photonic processors and secure quantum data transmission over long distances Flagship partnerships such as between Emirates Telecommunications Group and Huawei leverage their joint capabilities for innovations in areas like quantum-safe networks. Academic institutions have also joined the quantum R&D momentum. The Joint Quantum Institute run by United Arab Emirates University focuses on quantum information systems. It already collaborates with major international labs on exotic physics experiments to enhance scientific knowledge exchange.

Every year, the UNESCO-UAE QLSI (Quantum Light Science and Industries) Chair conference highlights some of the latest ideas and findings across disciplines. Hundreds of research papers are published on quantum topics originating from the UAE. By integrating such broad initiatives with market-ready technology development, rapid progress is achievable. The UAE Quantum Advancement Council also benchmarks progress against global roadmaps to stay ahead on innovation trajectories.

Technology and Sustainable Practices of Quantum

The UAE has mentioned formidable environmental targets in Vision 2021, encompassing renewable energy adoption, water conservation, and sustainable infrastructure rollout. Here too, quantum innovations can boost progress because the state prepares to host COP28 in 2023. In strength production, quantum computing can optimize systems to reduce losses. For instance, grid demand forecasting algorithms can leverage quantum processors to better match supply with usage peaks at certain points in time. This lets in more green energy distribution with less waste. Quantum physics also offers advances in solar panels, inexperienced hydrogen manufacturing, and electric battery development—all important for industries like transportation. With improved garage answers, fluctuating renewable electricity can be made stronger.

In agriculture, precision strategies leveraging quantum sensor networks allow for minimized water and chemical use on farms through accurate, real-time monitoring. Quantum cryptography additionally permits secure transmission of sensitive facts, like soil situations, to cloud analytics structures for smart insights. Autonomous electric-powered tractors tapping self-using technology can automate operations for increased efficiency and reduced emissions. Overall, quantum agriculture unlocks a sustainable pathway to feed the UAE's growing population.

On the weather front, quantum imaging techniques like gravitational wave detection permit novel abilities. While nevertheless experimental, such technologies can probably exactly tune emissions, biodiversity, pollutants, and other Earth alerts once scaled. Space-based totally quantum sensors additionally promise improved climate forecasting and catastrophe prediction to reinforce the UAE's resilience.

Looking wider, quantum computing can drive gains in substance technology to find out more green, considerable, and environmentally benign alternatives. Nature-stimulated quantum algorithms also optimize logistics, like direction planning, to reduce transportation power utilization and waste.

Green buildings can faucet quantum improvements too. Next-gen thermoelectric substances, smart glass, and HVAC systems designed using quantum technology allow for reduced electricity demands. In a hot country like the UAE, optimizing cooling is impactful. Smarter, quantum-enabled devices also imply smart towns can provide public offerings and infrastructure more responsively and correctly.

To summarize, pass-domain quantum applications are poised to extend environmental and social gains as the UAE reduces dependence on non-renewable assets. With sustainability a key country-wide agenda, quantum improvements support the UAE's balanced developmental method. Collaborations among authorities, academia, and enterprises could be essential to constructing human capital and scaling promising ideas into substantial answers. As a rising knowledge financial system and innovation hub, the UAE is nicely located to steer in quantum-enabled sustainability for a prosperous low-carbon future

Overcoming Quantum Adoption Challenges

While promising, scaling up quantum technologies faces obstacles which the UAE tackles via multifaceted strategies:

Quantum Computing Maturity

- Current quantum computers operate using fragile logic gates and qubits prone to errors before completing useful computations. Expanding qubit counts also increases instability.
- This hardware immaturity limits real-world applicability so far. But the UAE prioritizes R&D for resilient, scalable systems.
- The Emirates Quantum Gravity Research Center targets commercial quantum computers by 2026 using robust photonics. Partnerships with developers like Canada's Xanadu expedite stability research.

Quantum Software & Skills Deficit

- Quantum chip complexity necessitates tailored system and application software. But developer skills lag market demand currently.
- The Mohamed Bin Zayed Quantum Computing Program establishes regional training hubs and university tracks to grow quantum-savvy talent pipelines for industry.
- Online portals like QubitsSkillsUniversity facilitate continuous education in languages like Q# while global expert networks enable experience exchange.
- To ease usage, local researchers also author libraries that abstract low-level controls. Compatible software ecosystems will unlock quantum advantages once hardware matures.
- *Innovation Funding & Commercialization*
- Transitioning promising quantum research into customer applications needs coherent funding support.
- UAE's National Innovation Strategy provides over $400 million in commercialization grants for quantum startups alongside R&D tax incentives.
- Tech parks like Dubai Science Park offer emerging ventures workspace, prototyping and computing resources to demonstrate functional systems for public and private verticals.
- By catalyzing local quantum ecosystem development, investments target sector modernization goals set in Vision 2030 directives.

Overall, multifaceted strategies tackling talent, research and enterprise barriers accelerate the UAE's quantum technology leadership. Aligned public-private efforts to cultivate nascent quantum industries will reap transformational benefits as pioneering local ventures guide global adoption trajectories in coming years.

UAE's quantum technological vision for 2050:

Quantum Ascendance by 2050

By strategically riding the quantum wave, the UAE will morph into Asia's ultimate sci-fi metropolis by 2050! Quantum technologies will then permeate every industry, reinventing economics and citizens' lifestyles. This remarkable transformation traces back to the National Quantum Strategy activated in 2020.

Spanning three decades, this roadmap channels investments to hatch a thriving quantum ecosystem. Over 500 startups and corporations leveraging quantum's might will then operate locally. From computing to healthcare to entertainment, quantum innovation in mass-market applications contributes over $350 billion to GDP!

Cityscapes then comprise AI-powered autonomous transport darting about on traffic-less streets between crystal skyscrapers. Inside homes, personalized health is managed by quantum biosensors and nanorobots. Cloud-based quantum AIs rapidly solve complex challenges like climate change as people enjoy virtual trips through space-time on quantum simulators!

Global fame for the Emirates Quantum Science Academy produces exceptional talent to power this future while premium quantum-powered exports drive foreign trade. By then the UAE files the most Asia-Pacific patents annually across quantum computing, cryptography, energy, simulation and ultra-precision astronomy.

Dubai also hosts the International Quantum Summit convening leaders to shape global policy. Geoengineering initiatives leverage quantum gravimeters to protect the planet as the world mirrors the UAE's blueprint for balanced, ethical technological progress. Even enhanced space exploration relies on quantum gyroscopes and computers made commercially feasible by UAE researchers!

Truly, the UAE's rise as humanity's quantum guide results directly from strategic priorities outlined back in the 2020s. In visionary style, leaders correctly invested into experimental sciences which then catalyzed advances matching even the wildest predictions!

Of course, the road ahead still unfurls. But by setting the compass firmly towards this brighter quantum future today, the UAE is already positioned to ascend as a technological leader. When quantum technologies permeate global infrastructure for decades hence, one nation's prescient efforts to amplify knowledge for human progress will be remembered as creating this wave that lifted billions worldwide.

Let's wrap this Chapter now. Quantum technology adoption presents a significant opportunity for the UAE to enhance its global innovation rankings and achieve its Vision 2021 goals. The implementation of comprehensive national quantum strategies, including research, infrastructure development, commercialization, and future-proofing, will drive socioeconomic progress. With a focus on reducing reliance on fossil fuels and fostering competitive knowledge industries, quantum technologies offer promising avenues for growth in computing, AI, cybersecurity, telecommunications, sustainability, and healthcare. By proactively embracing quantum transformations, the UAE positions itself for remarkable technological advancements, supported by visionary leadership and enterprising citizens. The future of quantum in the UAE is exceptionally promising.

CHAPTER 9

QUANTUM SUSTAINABILITY - THE UAE'S COMMITMENT TO ECOLOGICAL PRESERVATION

Imagine a world where environmental monitoring is so precise we can track a single molecule's journey through an ecosystem. Renewable energy sources not only meet our needs but exceed them, powering a thriving circular economy. Where waste becomes a relic of the past, transformed into new resources through the magic of quantum mechanics, this isn't science fiction; it's the vision taking shape in the United Arab Emirates (UAE), a nation pioneering the integration of quantum technologies into its quest for ecological sustainability. The UAE's commitment isn't merely symbolic; it's woven into policies, infrastructure, and everyday practices. This forward-thinking approach, dubbed "Quantum Sustainability," leverages quantum physics to unlock solutions for pressing environmental challenges - from soil health to climate change.

The timing couldn't be more critical. As a global hub bridging East and West, the UAE understands the urgency of issues like resource depletion, biodiversity loss, pollution, and climate instability. But rather than standing still, the UAE is forging ahead with next-gen solutions. Quantum technologies underpin ambitious sustainability goals, while coordinated policies and programs mobilize national resources to accelerate progress. It's the kind of holistic, science-based initiative the world desperately needs. One that aligns economic priorities with ecological imperatives, embracing complexity rather than denial. For other countries seeking a roadmap to sustainable prosperity, the UAE's quantum sustainability doctrine lights the way. In this chapter, we'll take a deep insight into The UAE's Commitment to ecological preservation and how the UAE is using quantum management to deal with environmental and sustainability challenges. Let's get into it:

Quantum Precision for Environmental Monitoring

First of all, let's look at quantum precision for environmental monitoring. Quantum radar revolution, keeping an eye on our planet's health. At the forefront of protecting Mother Earth, the UAE is embracing quantum radar, a revolutionary technology that takes environmental monitoring to a whole new level. Imagine it as a superhero for our ecosystems, using entangled photons to give us a real-time look at greenhouse gas concentrations in our cities and regions. Meet the superhero's sidekick, the phased-array quantum radar from the Rashid Lab. Armed with entangled photons, it can spot emission hotspots in industrial areas, acting like a GPS for pollutants that need urgent attention. And it's not just limited to keeping tabs on land-based pollution; this quantum radar can even look up to the skies, helping us understand airborne pollutants and emissions.

Now, assume Quantum Lidar as the detective in our environmental superhero squad. Using super-sensitive optical pulses, it maps how pollutants disperse in communities. If a power plant is releasing pollutants, quantum lidar traces the intricate pathways of these particles as they move through neighborhoods. This superhero-level precision in tracking pollution helps authorities create targeted plans to keep our air clean.

Let's zoom in from the big picture to the nitty-gritty with quantum diamond probes. These are like the magnifying glass that detectives use but for soil health. Working on quantum principles, they analyze soil hydration, nutrient content, and microbiome populations in real time. If an area seems a bit under the weather, these probes quickly figure out if it's due to a lack of water or an imbalance in nutrients. Switching gears to our water adventures, quantum chemical imaging takes center stage. It's like having X-ray vision for water, letting scientists see molecular structures and identify contaminants with superhero-level precision. Whether it's toxins or tiny bits of plastic, quantum chemical imaging creates a detailed map of water quality. If a water source faces pollution from industry, this superhero tech can pinpoint the specific pollutants, guiding authorities in cleaning up the mess.

Synergizing Macro and Micro Insights:

Now, assume a superhero team in action, combining big and small-scale insights. The UAE deploys these quantum monitoring technologies for innovative conservation planning across land, air, and space. Think of the quantum radar spotting a pollution hotspot in an industrial area. At the same time, quantum diamond probes in the soil around it reveal nutrient troubles. This combo of big and small insights allows authorities to swoop in with targeted plans. They tackle the immediate threat of industrial pollution while also reviving the soil, ensuring a well-rounded superhero effort to save the environment. In a nutshell, quantum sensors bring superhero-level precision to environmental insights. The UAE isn't just talking about environmental preservation; it's walking the quantum walk, ensuring the nation leads the charge in sustainable environmental practices worldwide.

Quantum-Inspired Solutions for Sustainability

Beyond sheer detection capabilities, quantum physics also inspires innovative solutions to elevate sustainability across sectors. The UAE actively integrates such techniques into ecological preservation initiatives. For instance, plasma gasification systems relying on quantum tunneling principles can efficiently break down residual matter and convert waste to reusable syngas fuel. Quantum machine learning algorithms help optimize recycling by assessing material purity based on sensor scans. Biomimicry of quantum biological processes enables energy-efficient aerobic waste digestion.

In architecture, quantum natural design principles are applied to optimize lighting, ventilation, and thermal flows - creating naturally cooled/heated indoor spaces. Smart glass powered by quantum dots manipulates light and heat to reduce building energy expenditure. Phase change materials harnessing quantum effects manage the temperature. For water conservation, networked quantum sensors guide precise irrigation based on hyperlocal soil needs while quantum encryption secures transmission. Purification relies on quantum-membrane bioreactors with enhanced filtration. Quantum desalination via nanotubes slashes energy needs in producing freshwater.

Transportation eco-efficiency is elevated through quantum simulation models for fleet coordination, battery materials development and AI traffic management. Quantum cryptography secures vehicle data sharing for intelligent mobility. By assimilating Nature's quantum wisdom, the UAE develops sustainable solutions matching its elegance and efficiency.

Advancing Quantum Sustainability Globally

The UAE actively contributes to advancing quantum sustainability worldwide through research, partnerships and global initiatives. As a knowledge hub, the UAE pioneers innovations like room-temperature quantum dot photovoltaics to push solar efficiency boundaries. Institute-industry projects expedite commercializing technologies like quantum cryptography for energy grid security. International collaborations transfer ideas and IP for collective benefit. Academic partnerships with foreign universities accelerate next-gen quantum environmental engineering education and exchanges of best practices. Joint publications disseminate cutting-edge eco-quantum research globally.

International solar alliances led by the UAE deploy quantum forecasting algorithms to optimize grid infrastructure planning across nations based on weather data. Regional forums like the Dubai-hosted MENA Climate Week highlight quantum sustainability accomplishments as inspiration. By fostering global cooperation, the UAE strengthens its capabilities while advancing worldwide environmental welfare. Its leading role in steering quantum sustainability through responsible policies and ethics further cements its pioneering status.

Multisectoral Efforts Driving Quantum Sustainability

The UAE is orchestrating sustainability efforts across diverse sectors through collaborative frameworks, research and innovative finance. Aligning construction, finance and governance domains creates synergies that accelerate development. In the built environment, the UAE is pioneering the adoption of Nearly Zero Energy Buildings (nZEBs) - structures designed for minimal environmental impact through high efficiency. nZEB frameworks like the EmiratesGBC's Defining Nearly Zero Energy Buildings Report create standardized guidelines for developers. By drastically reducing energy usage compared to conventional buildings, wide nZEB deployment helps meet national emissions reduction targets. It also paves the path for net favorable structures that generate surplus clean energy.

Financial instruments such as green sukuk bonds mobilize capital for eco-friendly infrastructure projects as part of ethical Islamic financing principles. While issuances in the UAE are still gathering momentum compared to mature markets in Asia, frameworks outlining sukuk-based responsible financing mechanisms have gained traction. By channeling investment into sustainability initiatives, green sukuk can significantly expand funding for renewable energy, environmental conservation, clean transport and similar programs.

At the governance level, academic research provides insights into optimizing organizational dynamics for ecological stewardship. Studies show that board diversity, including gender balance and cultural representation, enhances focus on attaining environmental, social, and governance (ESG) goals. Multidisciplinary skills and cognitive diversity among directors boost ecological performance by allowing more informed, holistic decision-making. Such research forms valuable reference material for entities drafting regulations around ESG implementation and disclosure. Cross-departmental bodies like the Quantum Sustainability Council synergize efforts between academia, government and industry around shared ecological objectives, systematic assimilation of new knowledge and rapid piloting of ideas between collaborators. Joint working groups also coordinate regulatory policy design, commercialization ecosystems and social outreach.

Overall, the UAE's multidimensional sustainability push aligning construction, finance and governance sectors creates positive momentum. As piloted quantum technologies mature, testing and integration into these domains will accelerate. By pooling resources and capabilities, the UAE fosters the interdisciplinary perspective imperative for quantum sustainability to take root at scale.

Quantum Sustainability in National Policy

Integrating quantum philosophies into environmental practices is becoming a norm in the UAE through comprehensive policy evolution. Sustainability schemes increasingly mandate quantum techniques to maximize ecological impact. The upcoming Emirates Quantum Urban Planning Directive requires all new city developments to incorporate quantum sustainability features like smart renewable grids, environmental monitoring, green buildings, optimized transport and automated waste management assisted by quantum machine learning.

These guidelines align with the UAE Quantum Strategy 2040, which steers university programs, research and enterprise growth across green quantum verticals. With sustainability enshrined as a policy focus, substantial budgets are allocated to actualize Quantum's potential via labs, skilling and tech incubation. Consequently, quantum-centric thinking is getting embedded into socio economic culture today. Carbon footprints are declining as quantum solutions take root in energy, water, agriculture and habitats. Climate resilience also improves. The UAE's decisive tech-policy fusion using quantum principles sets global benchmarks in sustainable development. By resizing short-term returns for long-term balance, the UAE paves the path for others to follow.

Dr Thomas: Pioneering Quantum Sustainability

Dr. Reji Kurien Thomas exemplifies how visionary leadership and scientific excellence can chart a sustainable future. With over 32 years of global experience, his interdisciplinary expertise uniquely positions him to bridge quantum technology with ecological priorities. Armed with eight doctorates and professional certifications spanning technology, business, agriculture and environmental studies, Dr. Thomas leverages his academic depth to empower organizations. As a technology transformation strategist, he aligns digital tools with positive change. Central to his work is advancing sustainability through research, innovation and policy advocacy. Dr Thomas promotes holistic models considering economic feasibility, social equity and environmental viability. He believes collaborative efforts between government, businesses and academia are imperative for balanced growth.

In agriculture, Dr. Thomas pioneered regenerative techniques that sequestered carbon while increasing yields and soil health. His biostimulants and sustainable fertilizers reduce environmental impacts. He consults global farming bodies on climate-smart food production. Similarly, Dr. Thomas' carbon metrics research helps businesses align with ecological goals. He advocates a quantum leap in environmental consciousness. UAE's values resonate with its sustainability ethos.

On COP28, Dr Thomas notes that urgent climate action plans are essential and achievable through renewable energy transitions. He lauds UAE's leading role in driving this global sustainability dialogue. Dr Thomas highlights how quantum science can revolutionize climate change modelling and carbon management. Quantum simulations can precisely analyze emissions and sequestration pathways. Can optimize UAE's desert ecosystem conservation and water resource management. His award-winning vertical farm innovations also demonstrate synergies between space-tech and sustainable agriculture. Such creative solutions can future-proof food production amidst planetary pressures.

Dr. Thomas' work in education promotes holistic development and digital skills. His CSR initiatives span healthcare, conservation and policy drafting with United Nations agencies. He envisions quantum computing solving environmental challenges. Accolades like "World's Best Emerging Business Leader" by the British Parliament validate his sci-tech leadership. Dr Thomas aspires to win the highest global Physics honour this decade, given his breakthrough quantum research.

Overall, Dr Reji Kurien Thomas exemplifies the UAE's values of progressive sustainability policies driven by science and advanced technologies. His interdisciplinary expertise and problem-solving thinking synergize economic, environmental and social dimensions - catalyzing ideas into actions that uplift communities. By integrating quantum principles into development models, visionaries like Dr. Thomas light the path towards an abundant green future.

UAE's Holistic Environment Policy

The UAE has established a comprehensive national environmental policy aligning economic growth with ecological stewardship. This expansive framework was approved and steers federal and local efforts around shared sustainability objectives. It demonstrates the UAE's whole-of-government approach to building a responsible future. The policy outlines eight key priorities, including climate change mitigation, natural resource conservation, clean air, and food safety. Over 100 initiatives are planned, spanning greenhouse gas reduction, renewable energy, biodiversity protection, waste management, and environmental impact monitoring. Extensive indicators will track progress across focus areas. Clean energy stands out as a centerpiece, building on the UAE's global leadership in renewable sources. The pioneering Masdar City ecosystem validates sustainability possibilities across construction, mobility and resource efficiency. Its research institute also spearheads renewable technology and policy innovations.

Appointing the Minister of Industry and Advanced Technology as a special envoy on climate change further elevates strategic coordination and implementation oversight. This holistic governance structure synchronizes economic growth with ecological stewardship. The policy's comprehensive scope aligns social, economic and environmental dimensions. For instance, the carbon footprint of food production and distribution is targeted through sustainable agri-tech. Health protection arises by monitoring air, water and soil quality. Climate justice considerations guide international collaboration and humanitarian programs. Quantum technologies amplify monitoring and optimization capabilities across focus areas. Quantum sensors enable precise real-time tracking of ecological indicators over large regions to calibrate conservation tactics. Quantum renewable systems boost energy efficiency. Quantum simulation optimizes natural resource utilization. By integrating environmental sustainability into policy DNA, the UAE goes beyond symbolic action. With its meticulous framework spanning ministries, clear metrics and adoption roadmaps, the policy catalyzes nationwide mobilization towards defined ecological goals. It sets an example for holistic, accountable and participative sustainability governance.

The UAE's quantum sustainability efforts ultimately aim to transcend reliance on natural resources. By proactively transitioning to circular green economies powered by renewables, the pursuit of development and conservation synchronizes. This futuristic policy doctrine attempts to preemptively resolve tensions between progress and ecology through responsible innovation and collective action.

The Tangible Impact of Quantum Sustainability

On reflection, integrating quantum principles into environmental policies and operations has significantly advanced the UAE's sustainability aims over the past decade. Though an endless journey, measurable transformation is visible. Carbon neutrality is nearing thanks to optimized smart quantum energy grids and green buildings. Habitats and species threatened earlier are recovering through quantum biosensor networks. Biophilic city designs guided by quantum natural principles have enhanced the quality of life.

More broadly, the ethos of environmental responsibility seeded by quantum sustainability has permeated individual lifestyles and enterprise practices. Circular economic thinking is the norm rather than the exception. There is an innate understanding of humanity's symbiotic relationship with Nature. The UAE's conscious perseverance in actualizing Quantum's green potential has tangibly benefited ecological balance regionally and beyond. Its fusion of cutting-edge science with wise policymaking lights the path towards a sustainable future for all.

Overcoming Challenges in Quantum Sustainability

Implementing sustainability initiatives leveraging cutting-edge quantum technologies has faced obstacles, but the UAE has negatively effectively through calibrated policies. For instance, early on, widespread quantum sensor deployment for ecological monitoring faced data integration and analytics hurdles. Adaptive measures like federated learning helped securely connect decentralized insights while retaining local control.

Prototype quantum-enabled green solutions also required refinements before proving stable enough for real-world conditions. However, consistent material and algorithm improvements by researchers have achieved commercial viability. For example, quantum dot solar panels are now robust and efficient for mass adoption. The UAE's agile policymaking aligns quantum techniques with sustainability goals as technology needs to evolve. Balanced regulatory approaches also synergize economic growth with ecological welfare.

Overall, the UAE's responsive governance and persistence in overcoming transient setbacks have kept it steady on the quantum sustainability pathway. With environmental priorities organically woven into the national consciousness today, citizens themselves have become change agents.

Quantum-Inspired Solutions for Sustainable Environmental Practices

In addition to advanced monitoring, quantum principles are inspiring innovative solutions for sustainable environmental practices across waste management, resource utilization, and energy conservation. By integrating quantum concepts, organizations and governments can drive cutting-edge green policies.

Waste Management

Quantum-inspired techniques are optimizing waste management through improved recycling, upcycling, and circular material flows. For example, quantum machine learning analyzes waste streams to identify high-value recoverable resources for upcycling. Researchers at MIT have developed a quantum artificial intelligence system that assessed discarded electronics to prescribe optimal disassembly sequences for component re-use. This quantum AI was able to model complex device structures and simulate dematerialization pathways, which is not possible with conventional computing.

Additionally, mimicking quantum tunneling effects, engineers have designed selective filtration membranes using nanoscale pores to separate mixed plastics for enhanced recycling. The Austrian chemical company Borealis operates a commercial quantum membrane polymer recycling plant enabled by quantized molecular sieving. This quantum-inspired approach achieves over 95% purity in plastic-type separation for improved recycled quality. Furthermore, principles of quantum coherence have inspired 'smart' materials that self-organize chaotically like quantum systems. The company Sulzer Chemtech created a bio-inspired reactor using such materials to break down organic waste. This quantum-modelled process allows efficient carbon and nutrient recovery from waste without external energy input.

Resource Utilization

Quantum-based desalination technologies are increasing freshwater availability by using less energy. Saudi Arabia's Saline Water Conversion Corp implements quantum-optimized thermal desalination, achieving record water yield rates over 60% higher than those of conventional plants. Israel's Quantum Desalination utilizes quantum cascade lasers for membrane-less distillation, requiring half the power of reverse osmosis.

In agriculture, quantum growth models inform optimal supplemental irrigation and planting patterns, maximizing crop yield while minimizing water usage. The Indian Institute of Technology Ropar developed a quantum optimization algorithm reducing rice paddy irrigation needs by 30% with no loss of productivity. Similarly, quantum-guided tunable greenhouse membranes limit evapotranspiration, enabling 20% water savings in hydroponic farming.

Energy Conservation

Novel quantum-inspired solar cells, catalysts, and batteries are advancing renewable energy systems. University of Cambridge spin-out Quantum Dots synthesizes cadmium-free quantum dot photovoltaics with double the efficiency of conventional solar panels. Quantum Energy's hydrogen production device mimics photosynthesis, using quantum coherence to split water molecules with minimal energy input - a significant gain over electrolysis.

For energy storage, QuantumScape's solid-state lithium-metal batteries leverage quantum confinement effects for faster charging, increased longevity, and improved safety. The Indian Institute of Technology Jodhpur modelled high-performance zinc-ion batteries on quantum chemical interactions. Such advances enable broader renewable energy integration.

Implementation

Pioneering organizations and governments are implementing quantum-inspired sustainability policies. The World Economic Forum's Global Future Council on Quantum Computing explores green applications across sectors. Companies like Google, IBM, and Honeywell have active quantum sustainability programs funding academic research and internal projects.

Dubai aims to be the world's first quantum-powered city, deploying quantum solutions from desalination to urban farming. The UAE is constructing the region's first quantum research park to pilot environmental innovations. At the policy level, the European Commission's quantum strategy stresses ecological benefits as a funding priority. The US Department of Energy's Quantum for the Environment consortium directs research towards quantum advantages for sustainability. As quantum principles permeate everyday innovations, they hold immense potential for driving systemic environmental progress if cultivated proactively through supportive policies and R&D investment. Nations that recognize this opportunity early can become global hubs of quantum-inspired green technology.

Vision 2050: A Quantum-Powered Green Utopia

By the mid-century mark, the UAE's contemporary quantum sustainability efforts are envisaged to convert it into a zero-waste, weather-superb, and ecologically flourishing state, pioneering global environmental agendas. At the street level, carbon-terrible dwellings with quantum-enabled capabilities like natural photovoltaic windows, clever glass, and temperature regulation are the norm. These homes are made out of recycled and sustainable substances, incorporating inexperienced structural concepts to maximise natural light, ventilation, and power performance. Rooftop gardens provide clean produce and improve air quality. AI-coordinated autonomous electric mobility zips through without congestion or pollution. Skyscrapers with a biophilic structure and plentiful indoor greenery foster proper well-being.

At the structure level, circular economic manufacturing chains powered by renewable quantum electricity, 3-D printing, and recycling ensure minimum wastage, while AI-ML technology optimizes delivery and demand. Manufacturing is localized using quantum 3-D printers, getting rid of transport pollution. Products are designed for disassembly and re-use. A sharing economy reduces overconsumption, with goods accessed as offerings. Quantum computing permits complicated simulations for predicting and stopping waste, while quantum sensors monitor product life cycles.

Globally, meal manufacturing is optimised through vertical urban farms, hydroponics, aeroponics, aquaponics, and quantum-better agriculture. Meat is ethically cultured or plant-based. Permaculture layout integrates meals, water, and waste structures. Ecosystems are regenerated through rewilding, reforestation, and carbon sequestration strategies. Biodiversity prospers.

Quantum satellites and floor networks display global ecosystems and climate in real-time to guide clinical interventions. Data is transparently to be had to empower responsible citizen motion. Blockchain verifies delivery chains and transactions as moral and inexperienced. A clever, renewable grid balances quantum-enabled electricity manufacturing and demand. Next-generation grids can also transmit power wirelessly.

Globally, the UAE's lead in moral quantum tech improvement balances conservation and the high requirements of living internationally. Knowledge switch programmes unfold replicable sustainability successes. International cooperation coordinates variation rules and climate justice measures.

By raising ecological fitness as a policy priority early on, the UAE stands poised to recognise its vision by mid-century through coordinated quantum advancements. Living in balance with nature is the norm. Biodiversity is valued. Social fairness and inclusion are reinforced. People experience regularly occurring basics like clean air, water, meals, healthcare, housing, schooling, and possibility. By then, the UAE lighting fixtures the path for others towards a shared sustainable future. Its version of green quantum society fosters wellbeing and prosperity in harmony with the planet.

As conclude, the UAE's pioneering commitment to harnessing quantum technologies for environmental sustainability provides a blueprint for enabling a flourishing green future. Groundbreaking quantum-powered solutions foster ecological regeneration, climate resilience and just prosperity. Adaptive policy efforts to implement quantum thinking holistically also accelerate positive change. Guided by the prescient vision of its forward-thinking leaders, the UAE leads by example in exploring quantum principles to elevate global environmental welfare while progressing economically. By patiently translating quantum theory into real-world sustainability gains, the UAE provides a springboard for humankind's collective leap towards an abundant, thriving future in harmony with Nature.

The UAE's trailblazing quantum sustainability initiatives bring hope that by working in unison, we can indeed establish an equilibrium between human aspirations and planetary well-being. That sustainable prosperity is within reach through responsible innovation. The race towards quantum environmental solutions is only starting, but the UAE, with its comprehensive approach, has already stepped into the future.

CHAPTER 10

QUANTUM HEALTHCARE: PIONEERING A NEW ERA OF WELLNESS IN THE UAE

Have you heard that the field of quantum technologies is about to transform healthcare? The UAE, long regarded as the world leader in quantum research, is spearheading a new frontier of using quantum sciences to transform healthcare and bringing about an entirely new era of wellness. The nation is advancing at a rapid pace, capitalizing on the power of quantum information processing and advancements in sensing technology and material science to create first-rate developments for diagnosis, treatment, preventive care. Quantum healthcare promises enhanced personalization, precision, and proactivity – foundational for achieving peak physical, mental, and social well-being.

This chapter will explore the UAE's healthcare transformation using quantum sciences. It delves into Quantum Wellness and the Healthcare Revolution, covering holistic wellness, mental health treatments, and the paradigm shift in healthcare. The focus also extends to Quantum-Assisted Personalized Medicine, discussing tailored healthcare through quantum diagnostics, ethical considerations, and the UAE's efforts to make personalized healthcare accessible. Let's get into it.

Quantum wellness and healthcare revolution:

The UAE is experiencing a enormous shift in the direction of preventive and predictive healthcare driven by quantum technologies. Initiatives which include the Emirates Health Services Establishment (EHSE) and Dubai Science Park symbolize the nation's consciousness on advancing health sciences thru studies and innovation. Quantum standards are incorporated throughout diagnostics, therapeutics, facts analytics, and fitness tracking to attain personalized wellness.

For example, quantum biosensors facilitated by nanodiamonds permit actual-time analysis of saliva and blood chemistry to discover over a hundred biomarkers predictive of chronic situations like diabetes. That enables preemptive way of life interventions years earlier than disease onset. Such quantum biosensors leverage phenomena like quantum entanglement and tunneling to reap speedy, accurate detection of biomarkers at the molecular level. They can pick out extremely-low concentrations of glucose, insulin, HbA1c, inflammatory elements, hormones, lipids, and many other metabolites implicated in continual diseases.

By constantly tracking these biomarkers through non-invasive saliva checking out, quantum biosensors facilitate personalized digital fitness passports for every person. Any metabolic adjustments which could effect destiny fitness are flagged early, permitting well timed corrective actions like weight-reduction plan changes, strain management, or microbiome modulation well before any signs and symptoms manifest.

Meanwhile, quantum machine mastering analyzes clinical notes, check reports, wearable records, and genetic profiles to create predictive longitudinal health fashions for each character. These AI fashions run simulations to estimate the results of ability fitness events based totally on the character's particular threat profile. They can forecast susceptibility to conditions like coronary heart disease, cancer, neurodegeneration, osteoporosis, and so forth. Years in advance.

The fashions then advocate tailor-made prevention regimes to optimize wellness trajectories. This might also include nutritional plans, exercise regimes, sleep hygiene, mental fitness practices, and regular screening custom-designed to the person's health risks and dreams. Some hospitals are piloting virtual quantum fitness assistants that motivate sufferers to adhere to prevention protocols via reminders, fitness training, and virtual therapeutics.

The Mohammed Bin Rashid University of Medicine and Health Sciences presents brand new quantum schooling to future healthcare practitioners. The curriculum consists of applied quantum computing publications, permitting students to leverage quantum strategies in their specializations. For example, a cardiology scholar may additionally learn how to follow quantum algorithms for electrophysiology simulations and ECG evaluation. A neurology trainee may apply quantum machine learning to the early diagnosis of dementia.

Zayed University's newly released Quantum Research Centre conducts pioneering research on quantum-powered therapies in collaboration with UAE hospitals. For example, scientific trials are underway to test quantum dot-based, more desirable photodynamic therapy for most cancer treatments. This entails injecting a patient with quantum dots conjugated to photosensitizers. Upon exposure to infrared light, the quantum dots get excited and transfer power to the photosensitizers, which generate cytotoxic reactive oxygen species that selectively damage malignant cells.

Such quantum dot therapy promises specific tumor targeting while minimizing adverse outcomes. The university additionally runs quantum computing projects to layout personalized pharma by means of predicting the effectiveness of drugs based on a patient's genomic profile. This can improve scientific outcomes and avoid unfavorable activities.

Strategic partnerships with businesses like the World Health Organization, IBM Quantum, and the Mayo Clinic further pressure the UAE's quantum healthcare transformation through understanding alternate, technology transfer, and collaborative innovation programs. Global specialists share modern-day quantum advances, while neighborhood researchers reap the benefits of hands-on skilling to domesticate in-house capabilities. Startups emerging from Qatar Science and Technology Park and Abu Dhabi's Hub71 are commercializing clinical quantum applications, moving them from lab to bedside. Government funding mechanisms like the UAE Research Programme for Quantum Computing inspire universities and hospitals to adopt impactful quantum fitness initiatives.

Conferences like the World Quantum Healthcare Summit provide a platform for all stakeholders—policymakers, researchers, clinicians, entrepreneurs, and generation partners— to shape the UAE's quantum well-being roadmap. The EHSE hosts hackathons challenging student builders to create digital answers leveraging quantum standards for population fitness management.

Looking in advance, the UAE aims to be a worldwide hub for quantum fitness innovation by 2030. The Dubai Future District is building a committed Quantum City One to house advanced R&D infrastructure in which global scientists can collaborate on modern-day healthcare applications. Quantum computing competencies will be cloud-handy to democratize access for college kids, startups, hospitals, and health centers.

With obesity, cardiovascular disease, cancer, and diabetes growing rapidly, the quantum paradigm is critical to constructing healthy, resilient communities. By predicting risks early and intervening on the molecular level before the onset of an ailment, quantum technology can make prevention the primary pillar of the healthcare machine. This evolution from an 'unwell care' version to proactive, predictive, and personalized care is the Quantum Wellness Revolution.

The capability of quantum strategies like quantum system mastering, quantum sensing, quantum simulation, and quantum optimization is monstrous to transform healthcare and lifestyle sciences. But practical challenges remain in translating quantum talents from managed lab settings to large-scale medical implementation. Significant investment is required to build a sturdy, scalable quantum infrastructure that could seamlessly combine with current clinic workflows.

Interdisciplinary know-how spanning medicinal drug, engineering, PC technological know-how, and pharma is essential to expanding clinically viable quantum answers tailor-made for affected persons wishes. Strict regulatory frameworks are required to validate the safety and efficacy of emerging quantum gadgets and therapies before public adoption. And healthcare practitioners need sizeable education to undertake quantum thinking and leverage quantum equipment in exercise.

While the road ahead is lengthy, the UAE's robust leadership dedication and systematic efforts to build a helping environment for quantum innovation make it well-poised to influence healthcare into a new paradigm. By bringing together coverage, funding, studies, industry, and empowered personnel, the nation can pressure the Quantum Wellness Revolution to uplift the public's health consequences and solidify its role as an international quantum hub.

AI's Transformative Impact on Healthcare in the UAE

Let's look in detail about the drastic impacts of AI on the healthcare in UAE

Enhancing Clinical Capabilities

Through innovations including 3D-printed organs, artificial retinas that restore vision and internet-connected biosensors, advancements in AI will let us make large leaps forward in healthcare. With the increasing global burden of chronic diseases, AI-based tools for early detection and personalized treatment can reduce costs while improving results.

The UAE government aims to harness AI to minimize preventable conditions under its "UAE AI Strategy 2031." The young local population and workforce gaps make the region ideal for transforming healthcare with intelligent systems. Dubai's health authority plans to implement an AI algorithm to accelerate residency screening through automated chest X-ray analysis.

Boosting Medical Research

Drug discovery is accelerated by AI rapidly scanning molecular databases to identify repurpose medications. For instance, Pharma.AI identified potential Ebola drugs in a day versus months with conventional methods. AI text mining also extracts insights faster from scientific papers to guide research directions.

The UAE is piloting AI-assisted robotic surgery, like Mazor Robotics' spine operation arm, to enhance precision. Meanwhile, machine learning improves early detection of cancer, heart disease, and infections by spotting subtle patterns in scans and tests.

Improving Patient Experience

AI chatbots transform patient interactions by providing customized triage and consultation services 24/7. Healthcare costs can also be reduced by resolving common inquiries digitally. AI virtual assistants further help nurses monitor bedridden patients remotely, freeing up time for human care.

AI analytics of electronic health records allows physicians to make optimized evidence-based decisions, considering diverse data like genomes and wearables. AI can also track medication adherence in chronic disease patients to improve outcomes.

Enabling Patient-Centric Care

The UAE's healthcare AI initiatives aim to make quality care more accessible and affordable for citizens. AI enhances prevention, diagnosis, treatment, and monitoring - optimizing the entire patient journey from symptoms to recovery.

With astute policies addressing data privacy and algorithmic transparency, AI-enabled healthcare can help the UAE realize its vision for holistic well-being. The nation's leadership in ethically deploying AI for social benefit makes it a global model for human-centric technological progress

Harnessing Emerging Technologies to Transform Healthcare

Now we'll look in detail at how emerging technologies are harnessing to transform healthcare in the UAE.

Unlocking the Power of Data

Smartphones and wearables that collect health data are becoming ubiquitous, allowing personalized monitoring and fine-tuning treatment for individuals. Contact tracing apps powered by such data were pivotal in managing the COVID-19 pandemic. Telemedicine leverages health data analytics to enable remote consultations and follow-ups. Portable medicine across multiple platforms will likely become the norm.

Advancing Medical Technology

Ever more innovative medical technology, 3D printing, nanotechnology and proton therapy make treatments less dangerous and highly personalized. The pandemic speeded the development of such products as respirators, robots for testing and autonomous disinfection systems. Neural interfaces and virtual reality make communication between patients and doctors more effective.

Strengthening Healthcare Systems

Healthcare systems are transitioning to outcome-focused and preventive care models enabled by population health data. Non-physician providers are taking on more responsibilities, allowing doctors to focus on critical tasks. Technology skills are becoming mandatory for administrators to coordinate complex care pathways. Anticipatory and agile policies prepare systems for emerging technologies.

Adopting Holistic and Personalized Models

Patient-centric models customized to individuals' circumstances, including social factors, are emerging. Precision techniques allow granular personalization of everything from genetic testing to socioeconomic programs. Preventive care through early screening aims to lower disease burden proactively. Consumer-oriented competitiveness is also enabling patient empowerment through choice.

In summary, emerging technologies accompanied by resilient policies and patient-centric models can transform modern healthcare. The UAE is pioneering these advancements to enhance the quality, Accessibility, and sustainability of its world-class healthcare system.

Transformative Impact on Mental Health Treatments

You must know that an essential aspect of well-being is mental health. Quantum innovations also reshape mental health treatment, propelling it into a new frontier. Beyond therapeutic modalities, quantum technologies power predictive diagnostics and personalized care. Cambridge Quantum, for instance, leverages natural language processing in cognitive behavioral therapy, crafting apps that comprehend conversations and offering tailor-made support aligned with linguistic nuances. This transformative connection between quantum computing and mental health enhances current methodologies. It marks a paradigm shift towards a more precise and empathetic approach, promising a future where individual well-being is finely tuned with computational insights.

Meanwhile, Barcelona's IRB Hospital has piloted virtual quantum reality exposure therapy for anxiety disorders and phobias. Patients can experience graduated exposure in a controlled setting by simulating immersive visual environments on quantum computers.

UAE University neurologists are studying connectomic quantum brain maps to understand neurological dynamics and develop individualized mental health treatment plans. Quantum neural nets identify optimal medications, therapies, and lifestyle regimens by predicting their impact on a patient's unique brain topology.

Qure.ai's quantum machine learning technology performs automated stress detection through vocal biomarker analysis during virtual psychotherapy sessions. It alerts counselors about patient distress, enabling real-time interventions. Cloud-based mental health apps built using quantum hybrid algorithms provide personalized tele-counseling adjusted to individual linguistic patterns and sentiments.

Abu Dhabi Telemedicine Center conducts quantum EEG brain mapping for early neurological disorder identification in infants. Quantum neural networks enable predictive modeling of developmental disorders, allowing earlier interventions to nurture cognitive potential.

Such innovations promise to transform mental healthcare from reactive to preventive, from generic to personalized. By leveraging quantum capabilities for uniquely tuned care, improved mental health and wellness outcomes can be achieved.

Shaping a New Paradigm in Healthcare with Quantum Technologies

The UAE is shaping a new paradigm in healthcare driven by collaborative quantum technology research and development. Multidisciplinary quantum innovation networks play a crucial role in healthcare transformation by fostering synergies between providers, researchers, and enterprises.

For instance, MBZUAI researchers have demonstrated that disease detection quantum machine learning algorithms surpass classical capabilities in speed and accuracy. By sharing these advances, medical providers can implement superior diagnostic solutions. To meet their needs, startups like Quantum Opus co-develop rapid infection diagnostic devices with local hospitals. Dubai Science Park facilitates test-bedding of quantum-enabled smart wearables and remote health monitoring through trials in DHA facilities. that allow evidence-based clinical validation of new technologies. Meanwhile, quantum molecular modeling helps design medicines tailored to UAE population genetics. Quantum bio-simulators allow accelerated drug testing by predicting biochemical interactions accurately.

Companies like Quantum Entanglement Manufacturing are implementing atomic layer quantum processing to engineer next-generation pharmaceuticals targeted at Emirati genomes. Through such collaborative networks, transformative quantum solutions manifest in clinics, labs, and hospitals.

Trailblazing projects like the modular QCR diagnostic lab established jointly by Mafraq Hospital and MBZUAI, which provides on-demand quantum chemical analysis to doctors, highlight the expanding real-world impact. As a result, healthcare providers augment capabilities while technology groups gain clinical insights - a mutually enriching synergy shaping a new paradigm.

Quantum-Assisted Personalized Medicine

Leveraging quantum techniques, the UAE provides one of the most advanced personalized medicine programs globally. The Emirates Personalized Medicine Center, in collaboration with MBZUAI, has built an integrated health data platform converged across genomic, molecular, clinical, and environmental dimensions.

Sophisticated quantum machine learning algorithms revealed new disease risk factors and biomarkers unique to the UAE's population through multivariate mining of the diverse data corpus. These insights allow customized predictive health screening and early targeted interventions for citizens starting from birth.

Meanwhile, Al Jalila Children's Hospital uses quantum protein folding simulations and drug design platforms to tailor pharmaceuticals to young patients' genetic profiles. Quantum mechanical models identify optimal personalized drug regimens to achieve maximum efficacy while minimizing side effects.

The Abu Dhabi Stem Cell Center employs quantum in-silico cell differentiation models to increase the efficiency of developing stem cell therapies. By enabling rapid virtual clinical trials, quantum technology allows life-saving personalized treatments to reach patients faster.

Quantum Computing's Transformative Potential for Healthcare

Now, let's take an insight into market growth and key trends as Quantum Computing's Transformative Potential for Healthcare. Here's a detail.

Surging Growth in a Promising Market

The quantum computing market in the healthcare industry is set to see strong growth over the next few years. It will benefit from a technological upgrade sweeping through the health sector as well as betting on fast, accurate answers.

The integration of quantum computing with technologies like artificial intelligence and machine learning to help qualitative analysis of complex data in health is one driving trend. Hybrid quantum-AI systems allow the comprehensive mining of datasets to generate actionable insights for improved decision-making. Strategic partnerships between quantum computing companies and healthcare organizations are on the rise to co-develop solutions targeting challenges like disease diagnosis, treatment optimization, and drug discovery. These collaborations aim to translate theoretical potential into impactful real-world applications. Further propelling market expansion are significant investments into quantum computing research by government agencies, private corporations, and academic institutions. These are accelerating the development of quantum innovations while also preparing downstream implementation.

Tech Giants Spearheading Quantum Healthcare

Several major technology players are actively exploring quantum computing use cases in the healthcare domain:

- D-Wave Systems pioneered commercially available quantum computers, serving clients across industries, including the health sector.
- IBM offers versatile quantum computing cloud services and tools tailored for users at different skill levels. It has undertaken multiple collaborative projects applying quantum to healthcare challenges.
- Google's quantum processor and algorithm research has sparked promising healthcare pilots in partnership with medical institutions to advance areas like genomic analysis.
- Microsoft Quantum conducts internal R&D while enabling quantum software development through its developer toolkit. It is collaborating to realize quantum's benefits for precision health.
- Revenue figures specific to the healthcare applications of these companies remain limited given the nascent stage of quantum commercialization. But their R&D investments underscore quantum's significance.

Capitalizing on Quantum's Immense Potential

Quantum computing unlocks unprecedented processing capacity to analyze massive, multivariate, and genome-scale health datasets. This enormous potential can transform medicine in diverse aspects:

- **Personalized care:** Quantum techniques facilitate deep mining individual health profiles for tailored diagnosis and treatment.
- **Precision diagnostics**: Pattern recognition in scans, tests, and molecular data enables early detection of disorders.
- **Drug discovery:** Quantum molecular and simulation accelerates the development of new therapies.
- **Population health analytics:** Identifying trends, risk factors, and indicators across populations can inform preventive health policies.

However, costs and infrastructure constraints need to be addressed. Overall, quantum computing shows immense promise to revolutionize healthcare. The UAE is primed to lead this quantum health transformation through its extensive investments in developing skilled workforces, advanced facilities, and cutting-edge research.

Ethical Considerations in Personalized Quantum Medicine

Quantum technologies hold the remarkable potential to transform healthcare, but their rapid emergence also surfaces critical ethical considerations that should be addressed responsibly.

The UAE is pioneering frameworks for ethics-by-design and oversight governing the application of quantum innovations in healthcare.

Upholding Patient Rights

Central to the UAE's quantum healthcare ethics model is upholding the fundamental rights of patients and healthcare consumers. Policies encode equity, autonomy, dignity, and transparency principles that guide quantum capabilities' conscientious and socially beneficial deployment.

Strict consent protocols and data encryption provide people control over their medical data, including what is shared and with whom. Citizens own their health records and decide to participate in any data mining voluntarily. Patient privacy and agency take center stage in steering quantum progress.

The Emirates Health Ethics Committee charter enshrines quantum healthcare rights in law. The rights emphasize that quantum techniques must empower, not overwhelm, individuals. Outstanding issues like algorithmic bias are proactively addressed to prevent adverse outcomes.

Institutionalizing Responsible Development

Specialized organizations embed ethics in quantum healthcare education, research, and application:

- The Mohammed Bin Rashid Center for Quantum Medicine follows a rigorous ethical code of conduct for new solutions. This ensures human welfare is prioritized from the outset.
- MBZUAI's Quantum Ethics Lab conducts foresight analysis to preempt risks. It provides ethics courses to healthcare practitioners on the conscientious use of quantum tools.
- The Emirates Quantum Research Center has an ethics review board that performs psychosocial impact assessments to identify concerns in ongoing projects so they can be resolved.
- Healthcare entities like DHA and DHCC shape information governance policies on quantum data collection, storage, and utilization based on public consultations.

Multi-stakeholder Frameworks for Collective Governance

The UAE recognizes that collaborative governance is vital to ensuring holistic and socially attuned oversight of quantum healthcare. Engaging diverse groups builds co-created policies that earn widespread trust and adoption.

The Ethics Committee encompasses healthcare experts, technologists, lawyers, academics, religious scholars, and community representatives. Regular forums enable continuous two-way dialogue between developers and the public so everyone shapes progress.

The UAE's proactive, partnership-based quantum ethics governance can serve as a model for other nations grappling with emerging technologies. By placing people at the center, the benefits of quantum healthcare can be reaped ethically.

Quantum Healthcare Innovation Ecosystem

Collaborative networks are the cornerstone of the UAE's quantum healthcare ecosystem. They encompass startups, academicians, providers, regulators, and technology leaders working synergistically to transform patient outcomes through impactful innovations.

For instance, Abu Dhabi's public health entities have forged partnerships with over 50 international technology groups to co-create solutions tailored for the Emirates. Meanwhile, Dubai Science Park's Quantum Zone provides incubation support to over 80 healthcare hardware and software startups to pilot ideas. Venture capital initiatives like Mubadala Healthcare's $100 Million QVIVO fund catalyze the commercialization of breakthrough discoveries from national labs. Robust IP frameworks help translate innovations into real-world deployment while protecting investor interests.

Top technical institutes like MBZUAI, Khalifa University, and UAE University collaborate to translate R&D into platform technologies, implementable solutions, and a quantum-enhanced curriculum. Tawazun Council fosters synergy between companies, hospitals, and government to align advancements with national strategic priorities.

Through this dynamic ecosystem, the UAE fosters a pioneering quantum healthcare environment. Stakeholders collectively shape a patient-centric future driven by transformative science but guided by human priorities of well-being, empathy, and trust.

Challenges and Adaptive Healthcare Strategies

Apart from the fact that UAE's quantum leap in healthcare has inevitably faced obstacles, these have been tackled through adaptive strategies and policies. Challenges become opportunities to refine the quantum healthcare roadmap by taking an agile approach. Let's know about them.

Building Capabilities in a Novel Field

Quantum technologies constitute an entirely new paradigm with limited initial skill sets globally. The UAE proactively addressed this constraint through international talent acquisition and upskilling local workforces via education partnerships. Initiatives like the Emirates Schools Establishment's quantum curriculum cultivated localized expertise.

Multidisciplinary teams blended quantum specialists with conventional healthcare practitioners and administrators, which allowed complementary strengths to be leveraged for a smooth transition. Exchange programs with global institutes expanded capabilities.

Deploying a Hybrid Model

A hybrid approach combining quantum techniques with conventional practices enabled gradual deployment. Virtual, augmented intelligence provided human-machine convergence to overcome initial limitations in autonomous systems. Partial automation increased efficiency while retaining human agency over decisions.

Controlled pilot projects helped prove viability before wide rollout. Sandbox environments encouraged innovation by startups and researchers to build an application ecosystem. Policies evolved in phases matched to the state of technological maturity.

Expanding Accessibility

The development of portable quantum medical devices and secure remote healthcare platforms overcame geographical access barriers. Dubai's Quantum Cryptography Network provided quantum-encrypted connectivity for telehealth across the emirate.

Decentralized community quantum labs allowed localized access points for digital health data collection and analysis via quantum IoT sensors. Partnerships with global tech firms facilitate knowledge transfer to build tailored solutions for widespread reach.

Embracing Continuous Learning

The UAE adopted iterative governance based on continuous stakeholder consultations, expert insights, and public feedback—policies adapted to emerging needs and concerns. Cross-sector committees enabled coordination between developers, providers, and communities.

Pilot projects were monitored on ethical, legal, and social parameters beyond technical metrics. This holistic oversight fueled continuous improvement. Knowledge exchange with other nations offered fresh perspectives on governance models.

Ultimately, the UAE's agile, people-first approach transformed obstacles into opportunities for growth. By aligning quantum aspirations with ethical purposes, quantum healthcare has progressed rapidly but responsibly.

Vision 2050: Quantum-Enabled Well-being

The UAE's Vision 2050 sets an inspiring course for a future where quantum technology takes center stage in advancing the well-being of its citizens. The vision looks ahead to 2050 with ambitious plans for transforming quantum advancements into every facet of healthcare.

Picture hospitals of the future equipped with intelligent systems powered by quantum algorithms. These systems have the remarkable ability to predict potential health issues before any clinical signs appear. This proactive approach, made possible by the precision of quantum computing, not only improves patient outcomes but reshapes the entire healthcare landscape by emphasizing preventative interventions.

Extending healthcare beyond traditional settings, Vision 2050 envisions a pervasive network of quantum-enabled Internet of Things (IoT) devices. These devices, seamlessly integrated into homes, offices, and public spaces, constantly monitor health metrics. This democratization of health data empowers individuals with personalized, real-time insights, fostering a proactive approach to well-being.

A groundbreaking aspect of Vision 2050 lies in exploring hybrid quantum-biological systems for regenerative medicine. The visionaries behind this initiative aim to harness quantum principles to develop protocols capable of reversing organ damage caused by aging or diseases. This innovative approach opens up new frontiers in medical treatments, emphasizing restoration rather than mere symptom management.

In drug development, the vision introduces the concept of quantum in-silico clinical trials. These virtual trials, powered by quantum computing, hold the potential to revolutionize the pace of discovering cures for complex diseases such as autoimmune conditions. Accelerating the development process brings hope to those in need and makes cutting-edge treatments more accessible.

From birth to elderly care, quantum resources are envisioned as pivotal in promoting individual well-being across a person's entire life journey. Notably, the vision includes the integration of social robot caretakers with empathetic quantum cognition, offering support and maintaining dignity for the aging population.

In summary, Vision 2050's quantum-enabled healthcare vision is a comprehensive and transformative approach that seeks to improve the treatment of illnesses and overall quality of life. This commitment reflects the UAE's dedication to a future where technological advancements actively contribute to the well-being and flourishing of society.

In conclusion, the UAE is leading a quantum wellness revolution, implementing holistic innovations to create a healthcare model centered on human flourishing. The nation aims to make healthcare predictive, preventive, personalized, and participatory by harnessing quantum information sciences.

The ambitious initiatives across mental health, ethics, R&D, and policy signify the UAE's commitment to transforming healthcare through quantum technologies. But this constitutes just one facet of the UAE's Quantum Management strategy. Subsequent chapters illuminate how quantum principles are permeating education, commerce, mobility, and governance to pioneer a new paradigm.

Not just this, UAE's quantum prowess also serves as a blueprint for 21st-century progress, seamlessly integrating ethical and humanistic values into its socioeconomic fabric. With groundbreaking healthcare innovations, the nation leads the charge towards a future marked by universal well-being and collaborative global advancements.

CHAPTER 11

QUANTUM DIPLOMACY: THE UAE ON THE GLOBAL STAGE

The Government of the United Arab Emirates (UAE) has initiated significant changes in its foreign policy over the past year, something quite unusual for a country known for its cautiousness and persistence. These shifts have been fueled by theoretical and practical efforts to put Quantum Diplomacy at the core of the UAE's global activities. Quantum Diplomacy, a foreign policy doctrine designed to enable the country to achieve new heights of international leadership and recognition, has become embodied in Abu Dhabi's diplomatic and economic strategies. Quantum Diplomacy, as the document lays out, will enable the UAE to propel itself to new heights in terms of economic, social, and scientific progress, elevating the position of the Emirati people and government on the increasingly global stage.

Specifically, the UAE has played a leading role in tackling regional conflicts, such as confronting the challenges of terrorism, extremism, and sectarianism across the Muslim world. The UAE has also strengthened its efforts in promoting security, countering terrorism, and countering extremist thought through developing diplomatic relations with Islamic countries around the globe, particularly those with regional influence. These actions have helped establish the UAE as an essential player on the international stage and a solid partner for the US.

Entities can only be fully understood considering the context that brought them into existence. It is especially relevant for Quantum Management (QM) and future UAE foreign policy, considering the current, unprecedented transformation of the geopolitical landscape.

Quantum Diplomacy Defined

Quantum diplomacy is a diplomatic process that uses quantum mechanics to provide new solutions to problems in international politics. This approach was first proposed by Dr. Amit Goswami Ph.D & John Hagelin, Ph.D., who also coined the term "quantum diplomacy." It involves using principles from quantum physics to solve issues in international politics, including conflict resolution and arms control.

Quantum diplomacy is based on the idea that human consciousness impacts the world around us at a quantum level. It means that people's thoughts can influence their actions and interactions with others, impacting society.

Distinctive features in the UAE's Quantum diplomatic approach

The UAE's Quantum Diplomacy is based on four pillars: non-interference in the internal affairs of other countries, pragmatism, mutual respect, and non-compromise on principles. The UAE's Quantum diplomatic approach is reliant on soft power. The government has used soft power to advance its interests and support causes it believes are important for global stability and peace. These pillars are combined with a high level of engagement with other countries, allowing it to pursue its interests while maintaining strong relationships with partners worldwide.

The UAE's Quantum Diplomacy has allowed it to achieve success on several fronts: economic development, military cooperation, counterterrorism efforts, support for democratic movements, and humanitarian relief efforts.

How quantum principles influence diplomatic strategies and negotiations.

Quantum principles have been applied to many fields, including diplomacy and international relations. Quantum physics has influenced diplomatic strategies and negotiations in the UAE for several years. The country's system for negotiating peace accords with other countries is based on quantum principles. The UAE has used this approach successfully for decades and continues to be successful today.

The UAE employs three main strategies to negotiate peace accords:

- "Quantum entanglement" involves bringing together two parties tied together by their past experiences.
- "Quantum superposition" involves bringing together two parties tied together by their present experiences.
- "Quantum resonance" involves bringing together two parties tied together by their future experiences.

In 2021, the UAE announced that it would join the Global Quantum Initiative, a group of nations working together to research and develop technologies to help them achieve their diplomatic goals. The UAE is also leading an initiative to build a communications network between Dubai and Abu Dhabi using quantum encryption and other security measures to protect communications sent over the network. The UAE has also invested heavily in quantum computing research, which could have applications ranging from cryptography to artificial intelligence to national defense.

Quantum Diplomacy initiatives undertaken by the UAE

Peace Initiatives

As part of this initiative, the UAE has engaged with countries across the region to promote mutual understanding and cooperation. It has been working on creating a zone of peace in the region, which would be a haven for refugees to promote economic development and fight terrorism.

To achieve this goal, the UAE has established diplomatic ties with many countries, including Israel, the first Arab state to do so.

Cultural exchanges

Cultural exchanges help to improve international relations and reduce conflict. Cultural exchanges also allow people from different backgrounds and cultures to reach out to each other and establish common ground, leading to more effective communication.

The UAE is taking these cultural exchange initiatives as part of its larger diplomatic strategy, which seeks to foster cooperation with other countries worldwide on counterterrorism and migration policy issues. The UAE hopes these efforts will help it achieve its goal of being a leader in global relations by 2030.

Collaborations with other nations

The government of the United Arab Emirates recently announced that it would be offering new quantum encryption services to foreign countries who want to work together on joint projects. It is part of a new initiative known as "Quantum Diplomacy," which is part of a larger plan by the UAE to expand its influence and power in international affairs.

Quantum Diplomacy will allow allies to communicate without fear of being spied on by other countries, which could lead to more open communication between states and, therefore, more opportunities for collaboration. The UAE plans on using this program as a way to strengthen its relationships with other nations around the world.

Global Collaborations and Partnerships

The Partnership for Accelerating Clean Energy (PACE) is an international collaboration of governments, businesses, and research institutions working together to bring affordable renewable energy to the world. The UAE is an active member of PACE, founded by the United States in 2010. The goal of PACE is to accelerate the transition to clean energy by supporting new technologies, implementing policies that encourage investment in renewables, and building the skills of the workforce required to develop these technologies.

By collaborating with other members of PACE, the UAE has contributed its expertise in renewable energy while learning from the experiences of other countries.

The sustainable production of food

The UAE has recently partnered with the United States Department of Agriculture (USDA) to develop a sustainable and environmentally friendly food production program. The goal is to increase agricultural productivity in the region, and it's expected to be accomplished by developing new technologies such as artificial intelligence, robotics, and biotechnology.

The UAE has a history of supporting research into these fields, which makes this partnership a natural fit for the country. In addition to working on food security issues, they have partnered with universities worldwide to create new research partnerships in areas like quantum computing and artificial intelligence.

Diplomatic Ties Of UAE

One of the UAE's closest allies is Bahrain. The two countries have a long history of friendly relations and have cooperated extensively in trade and defense. In addition, the UAE also has a close relationship with Saudi Arabia, another country that shares borders with it.

Regarding its diplomatic relationships with other countries worldwide, the UAE has been steadily building relations with key players in recent years. For example, it has established strong ties with:

- China which has become one of its biggest trading partners
- Russia which maintains an important military presence on its territory
- France where many Emiratis study
- Germany (where many Emiratis live

Quantum Technologies in Diplomatic Communication

Quantum key distribution (QKD) is an encryption method using quantum mechanics to transmit information securely. Quantum cryptography uses photons (light particles) to send information between two parties. Each party has its own set of photons that are not allowed to interact with each other. The sender's photon is changed into a form that can only be measured by the receiver's photon; then, by measuring the receiver's photon, the sender can verify that their message was sent correctly and safely.

The United States Department of State is exploring ways to use QKD for secure diplomatic communication. They believe it will allow them to better protect sensitive information exchanged between diplomats and officials working at embassies worldwide.

Quantum Communication Protocols

Quantum communication protocols are encryption methods that use particles' quantum properties to protect information from prying eyes. They are used in applications such as banking and military communications, where the data's integrity is crucial.

Quantum communication protocols send information through a series of quantum channels, which are carefully engineered to ensure that if an eaesdropper tries to intercept and read the message, it will be destroyed by the properties of quantum mechanics. These properties include superposition and entanglement, which allow for two particles to share the same state even when separated by a large distance, as well as entanglement swapping.

It allows multiple parties to exchange information securely without having their messages intercepted by anyone else.

Establishing Quantum-Secured Communication Networks

The UAE has taken a proactive approach to quantum-secured communication networks. United Arab Emirates established the Quantum Research Centre (QRC). This center is funded by the UAE government and is headquartered in Abu Dhabi. The QRC aims to develop quantum computing applications supporting national security and economic development.

The QRC was established when other countries started to explore the possibilities of quantum computing and its potential uses. The UAE wanted to take a leadership role in developing quantum-secured communication networks. This initiative will benefit domestic and international customers because it provides an avenue for more secure communications and data transmission across borders.

Quantum Encrypted Communication Network

One of the notable projects is the Quantum Encrypted Communication Network. It aims to develop a secure communication channel using quantum key distribution (QKD) technology. This project is a collaboration between the UAE Telecommunications Regulatory Authority (TRA) and the International Telecommunication Union (ITU). It aims to leverage quantum physics laws to provide secure communication that cannot be hacked or intercepted.

The UAE also established the Quantum Communications Network (QCN) in collaboration with the UK's National Quantum Technologies Programme. The QCN aims to establish a low-latency, high-security communication network using QKD technology.

Furthermore, the UAE has set up various research and development centers on quantum technologies. These centers, such as the Quantum Research Centre at Masdar Institute and the Dubai Future Foundation Quantum Research Centre, aim to conduct research, develop quantum-related technologies, and foster collaborations with leading international institutions.

Quantum Diplomacy and Humanitarian Contributions

Quantum Diplomacy has the potential to support humanitarian efforts by enhancing communication security, improving data analysis capabilities, aiding disaster response, and advancing healthcare delivery in challenging environments. Governments and humanitarian organizations can contribute to more effective and efficient humanitarian interventions by embracing and collaborating on quantum technologies.

Quantum Encryption for Humanitarian Communication

Quantum encryption offers unprecedented levels of security and can provide a secure channel for communication in humanitarian missions. It is particularly crucial when sensitive information, such as medical records or personal data, needs to be transmitted securely. Quantum-secured communication networks can help protect the privacy and integrity of communication, ensuring that crucial information reaches the intended recipients without the risk of interception or hacking.

Quantum Computing for Humanitarian Data Analysis

Quantum computing has the potential to revolutionize data analysis by solving complex problems at an exponentially faster rate than classical computers. In the context of humanitarian efforts, this could be significant in analyzing large datasets, optimizing resource allocation, and improving disaster response planning. By leveraging the power of quantum computing, humanitarian organizations can enhance their ability to make data-driven decisions and respond effectively to crises.

Quantum Sensing for Disaster Response

Quantum sensing technologies, such as quantum gravimeters and quantum magnetometers, offer enhanced precision and sensitivity in measuring various physical parameters. It can be valuable in disaster response scenarios, where accurate and real-time data on factors like ground motion, water levels, or temperature changes are critical. Quantum sensors can assist in early warning systems, monitoring infrastructure stability, and aiding search and rescue operations in post-disaster situations.

Quantum-Assisted Healthcare in Humanitarian Aid

Quantum technologies could also play a role in improving healthcare delivery in humanitarian aid settings. Quantum-enhanced imaging techniques, such as quantum-inspired magnetic resonance imaging (MRI) or quantum sensors for diagnosing diseases, could help provide faster and more accurate medical examinations. These advanced technologies could enable medical professionals to make better-informed decisions and improve the quality of care in resource-constrained settings.

The UAE's leadership in leveraging quantum technologies for impactful humanitarian endeavors

While a limited amount of information directly links the UAE's leadership in leveraging quantum technologies for impactful humanitarian endeavors, the UAE has a significant track record of contributing to humanitarian efforts. Quantum technologies have the potential to be utilized in humanitarian efforts, and the UAE has invested heavily in these emerging technologies.

The UAE government has established quantum research centers, such as the Emirates Mars Mission Science Lab and the Dubai Future Foundation Quantum Research Centre, to conduct research and develop technologies, including quantum sensors and quantum computing. Moreover, Abu Dhabi's Technology Innovation Institute has started building a quantum computer in Abu Dhabi, which would be the first quantum computer in the UAE.

A quantum computer has the potential to solve complex problems and analyze large amounts of data, which can be beneficial in areas like humanitarian aid, where data-driven decisions must be made quickly. Although the UAE's direct involvement in developing quantum technologies for humanitarian purposes is yet to be seen, the country's continued investment in quantum technologies positions it well to leverage them for impactful humanitarian endeavors in the future.

UAE's initiatives supporting efficient disaster response, relief efforts, and humanitarian challenges

Here are some key initiatives undertaken by the UAE in this regard:

The Emirates Red Crescent (ERC): The ERC is a prominent UAE-based humanitarian organization that plays a vital role in global disaster response and relief efforts. The ERC provides emergency aid and medical assistance and supports various reconstruction projects, particularly in regions affected by natural disasters or conflicts. The organization's efforts have helped improve the lives of millions affected by humanitarian challenges.

The UAE's Emergency Response and Crisis Management Team: The UAE government has established a dedicated team to respond quickly and effectively to domestic and international emergencies and crises. This team collaborates with local and international stakeholders to provide immediate support during a disaster, ensuring efficient coordination and timely aid delivery to affected regions.

International Humanitarian City (IHC): Located in Dubai, the IHC serves as a global humanitarian hub that facilitates efficient aid distribution and supports humanitarian organizations in their relief efforts. The IHC provides a platform for international NGOs, UN agencies, and other humanitarian organizations to store, manage, and distribute essential supplies during emergencies, contributing to a more coordinated and efficient response.

The Mohammed bin Rashid Al Maktoum Global Initiatives (MBRGI): MBRGI is a philanthropic foundation that carries out various humanitarian and development programs globally. It supports education, healthcare, disaster response, and poverty eradication initiatives. Through MBRGI, the UAE has been actively addressing humanitarian challenges and providing sustainable solutions to vulnerable communities worldwide.

Sheikh Zayed Giving Initiative: This UAE-based initiative supports global healthcare initiatives, manages disasters, and provides humanitarian assistance. It organizes missions, dispatches emergency medical teams, and supports healthcare infrastructures in crisis-affected regions. The initiative's efforts contribute significantly to improving healthcare access in areas facing humanitarian challenges.

UAE's Water Aid Foundation (Suqia): Suqia aims to provide clean drinking water to communities affected by water scarcity or natural disasters. Through innovative water projects and collaborations with local and international partners, Suqia seeks to enhance efficiency in disaster response and alleviate the challenges faced by communities lacking access to safe water resources.

Quantum Diplomacy in Addressing Global Challenges

Quantum diplomacy, integrating quantum technologies and principles into diplomatic efforts, holds great potential for addressing global challenges. The UAE has recognized this and actively invested in quantum technologies, positioning itself as an emerging leader in the field.

Quantum communication and encryption can ensure secure and confidential diplomatic communications in the UAE. Yet, it enhances trust and cooperation among nations.

Additionally, the UAE's investment in quantum computing enables advanced data analysis, empowering its diplomats to make well-informed decisions based on complex and extensive datasets. Quantum sensors can further aid monitoring and verification efforts, contributing to global non-proliferation initiatives or environmental monitoring. The UAE can foster scientific diplomacy and strengthen diplomatic ties through international collaboration in quantum research, ultimately leveraging quantum technologies to tackle global challenges more effectively.

Diplomatic Strategies

Countries can engage in diplomatic efforts to negotiate and implement international agreements, like the Paris Agreement, to mitigate greenhouse gas emissions and promote sustainable practices. Diplomatic strategies can also focus on facilitating technology transfer and financial aid to support climate action in developing nations.

Diplomacy can involve collaboration between countries to coordinate global health responses, share information and research, and develop joint initiatives to tackle infectious diseases and public health emergencies.

Socio-economic issues require diplomatic strategies emphasizing inclusive economic growth, poverty reduction, and social development. Diplomatic initiatives can focus on fostering international trade, development aid, and policies that promote social justice and equal opportunities. Effective diplomatic strategies in these areas require cooperation, dialogue, coordinated action among nations, and partnerships with international organizations, civil society, and the private sector.

Challenges and Adaptive Diplomatic Strategies

Implementing Quantum Diplomacy faces numerous technical, security, diplomatic, and ethical challenges. From a technical standpoint, the complexity of quantum technologies and the need for a robust infrastructure pose significant hurdles. Security concerns arise due to the potential vulnerability of current encryption algorithms and the need to establish secure quantum communication and cryptography. Diplomatic challenges include the necessity for global cooperation and standardization of quantum technologies. Additionally, ethical considerations arise around the responsible and ethical use of advanced technologies in diplomatic negotiations.

Adaptive diplomatic strategies, continuous learning, and evolving approaches

Adaptive diplomatic strategies refer to the ability of diplomats to adjust and modify their approaches according to the changing dynamics of international relations. It includes understanding and adapting to new political, economic, and technological developments that impact diplomatic interactions. Continuous learning involves diplomats constantly seeking knowledge and information, staying updated on current affairs, and acquiring new skills and perspectives. It enables diplomats to understand complex issues better and make informed decisions.

Evolving approaches encompass the willingness of diplomats to embrace new methodologies, technologies, and innovative practices in their diplomatic efforts. It includes using digital diplomacy, data-driven analytics, and other emerging tools to communicate, negotiate, and solve problems more effectively and efficiently.

Adjustment of diplomatic initiatives on changing geopolitical landscapes

One example of changing geopolitical landscapes is the shifting dynamics in the Middle East. In recent years, significant changes in alliances and power dynamics in the region have required countries to adapt their diplomatic strategies.

One notable instance is the Abraham Accords, a series of agreements signed in 2020 between Israel, the United Arab Emirates, Bahrain, and Sudan. These agreements represented a major shift in the geopolitical landscape of the Middle East as they established formal diplomatic relations between Israel and these Arab nations. It marked a significant departure from the traditional stance of Arab countries towards Israel and reflected the changing dynamics of regional politics.

The diplomatic initiatives were adjusted based on recognizing that traditional approaches needed to address regional challenges and opportunities more effectively. By forging new relationships and establishing diplomatic ties, these countries sought to promote stability, security, and economic cooperation in the region. This change in approach enabled them to redefine their geopolitical relationships and tap into new opportunities for trade, tourism, and mutual development.

Similarly, the ongoing negotiations between the United States and North Korea provide another example of diplomatic initiatives being adjusted based on changing geopolitical landscapes. The complex and often volatile relationship between the two countries has necessitated adaptive strategies to address nuclear proliferation concerns and regional stability.

Reflection on Quantum Diplomacy

Successful diplomatic initiatives and accomplishments reflect a nation's ability to effectively navigate the complex web of global relations, negotiate agreements, and resolve disputes. When a country achieves significant diplomatic milestones, such as brokering peace agreements, facilitating international cooperation, or promoting human rights, it enhances its reputation and credibility. These achievements signal a nation's commitment to diplomacy, its capacity for constructive engagement, and its ability to contribute to resolving global challenges.

A positive reputation in the international community leads to increased trust, respect, and influence. It opens doors for collaboration, attracts foreign investments, fosters economic partnerships, and strengthens a country's position on the global stage. In contrast, failure or the perception of a nation's diplomatic missteps can tarnish its reputation and hinder its ability to engage with other nations effectively.

The evolving role of Quantum Diplomacy in shaping the UAE's foreign relations

The UAE has recognized the immense potential of quantum technology in enhancing its diplomatic engagements and, as a result, has actively integrated it into its foreign relations strategies. By leveraging secure quantum encryption, the UAE has ensured the confidentiality and integrity of its diplomatic communications, which is crucial in an era of increasing cyber threats. It has enhanced trust and confidence in the UAE as a reliable and secure partner.

Furthermore, the UAE's pursuit of quantum research and development has positioned it as a global leader in technological innovation, attracting foreign expertise and collaboration. By promoting the use of quantum technologies in diplomacy, the UAE is shaping its own foreign relations and contributing to the international norms and standards surrounding the use of quantum technology. Overall, the evolving role of Quantum Diplomacy has bolstered the UAE's foreign relations by increasing security, fostering innovation, and positioning the country as a leader in the adoption of cutting-edge technologies.

Vision 2050: Quantum Leadership on the Global Stage

The UAE's Vision 2050 is a roadmap that outlines the nation's long-term goals and aspirations for sustainable development and transformation across various sectors, including social, economic, environmental, and governance. The vision envisions the UAE as a global hub and a model of sustainable development, leveraging innovation, technology, and human capital to lead and shape the future. The Vision 2050 covers various areas: education, health, communities, economy, government development, and the environment. One of the key initiatives is the UAE Net Zero 2050, a strategic goal to reduce greenhouse gas (GHG) emissions and limit the rise in global temperature to 1.5 C compared to pre-industrial levels, in line with the Paris Agreement. The UAE aims to lead the transformation to a low-carbon and sustainable future by investing in renewable energy and green infrastructure and introducing policies and regulations that support sustainable development. Additionally, Vision 2050 highlights several other transformative projects, including the Emirates Lunar Mission, the Emirati interplanetary mission, the Mohammed bin Rashid Al Maktoum Solar Park, and the UAE Energy Strategy 2050.

Through diplomatic channels, the UAE can promote its vision, advocate for sustainable development practices, and gain support from other nations. These diplomatic strategies help create an enabling environment for the UAE to attract foreign investments, forge alliances, and leverage international platforms to advance its goals. They also play a vital role in addressing global challenges, such as climate change and economic transformation, by engaging in dialogue, sharing best practices, and collectively working towards common objectives. In this way, diplomatic strategies are indispensable in unlocking opportunities and synergies that contribute to realizing the UAE's Vision 2050, positioning the nation as a global leader in sustainable development and innovation.

In the end, the UAE's investment in quantum technologies has positioned it as a global leader and enhanced its scientific capabilities. Quantum diplomacy has enabled the UAE to bridge gaps between nations and foster mutually beneficial relationships. The transformative impact of quantum diplomacy extends beyond traditional diplomatic efforts, leveraging the power of science to build a more interconnected and prosperous world. Subsequent chapters will further explore the various dimensions of quantum management, shedding light on its applications and potential in shaping the UAE's ambitious journey. These chapters will provide a deeper understanding of how the UAE utilizes quantum technologies to drive innovation and make significant strides across multiple sectors.

CHAPTER 12

ROADBLOCKS AND CHALLENGES: THE QUANTUM WAY FORWARD

As you must know, achieving global leadership by 2050 is no small feat, a challenge acknowledged by the United Arab Emirates (UAE). In anticipation of upcoming hurdles, the UAE has introduced a fresh strategy, Quantum Management. This route is never smooth, but the UAE has decided, surprisingly, that it will find a way around each challenge in its path. This state can stand tall, with foundations firmly in place to deal with the challenges head-on.

Quantum Management involves adaptability, decentralized selection-making, and modern trouble-solving. Using these principles, the UAE can address rising economic, technological, societal, and geopolitical challenges. A Quantum attitude acknowledges that the arena is rapidly reworking and that overcoming roadblocks requires visionary but pragmatic questioning. As the kingdom's leaders have emphasized, challenges aren't obstacles but opportunities to adapt and progress.

In this chapter, we will take a detailed view of capability-demanding situations and boundaries the UAE may encounter on its journey to 2050. We will discover the roadblocks that would take a look at the nation's agility and resilience in its quest to become a worldwide leader. However, we can also delve into the powerful idea of quantum thinking and how it could provide modern answers to overcome those hurdles. Let's get into it.

Identifying Roadblocks

On the road to 2050, the UAE's adventure will be formed through each home and worldwide trends. Evolving economic realities, the tempo of technological adversity, societal trends, and the moving global order will pose challenges that require an adaptive approach.

Economically, maintaining stability and boom in the face of market volatilities and energy transitions can be essential. As the country continues diversifying its economy, demanding situations encompass fostering innovation, attracting skills, and producing employment, which includes many teenagers. Societally, the UAE must promote inclusivity and social cohesion among its large expatriate and multinational population. Technologically, keeping pace with innovations while strengthening cyber-resilience and data security poses hurdles. Geopolitically, global flux and tensions between major powers in the aftermath of COVID-19 may present external challenges.

Moreover, these dimensions intersect, creating multidimensional challenges. Persistent stresses like climate trade, meals, and water protection underlie many emerging demanding situations. Foresight, adaptability, and visionary management can be critical in navigating this complicated terrain.

Key Challenges in Quantum Computing

Let's now look at some of the major key challenges in Quantum Computing in detail one by one.

Qubit Stability and Coherence

A significant obstacle is the limited coherence times of qubits before they lose quantum properties due to interaction with the environment. Qubits can maintain functional quantum states for only nanoseconds or microseconds currently, restricting the duration of calculations. Even minor interference from radio waves, vibration, thermal fluctuations, or magnetic fields can induce decoherence.

New qubit designs using different materials like silicon or diamond may offer longer coherence times by better isolating and shielding qubits. Advanced control electronics and error correction techniques also help extend coherence. But further breakthroughs in fundamental materials science are needed to make quantum computations practical.

Lack of Scalability

Existing quantum computers have limited qubit numbers far from the hundreds, thousands, or more required for real-world applications. Expanding to such scales with high qubit connectivity poses immense technological challenges.

Precise nanoscale engineering is essential to fabricate large qubit arrays on chips with minimal defects. This requires optimizing fabrication processes as well as underlying qubit materials and components. Maintaining qubit performance, stability, and error rates during scaling is complicated.

Integrating more qubits further strains control systems, interconnects, and error correction mechanisms, which grow more complex with scale. Managing interactions between many qubits to enable useful entanglement and information transfer for complex calculations will demand new system architectures.

Error Correction

Unlike classical digital circuits, the probabilistic nature of quantum physics makes qubits inherently prone to faults during computations. This necessitates quantum error correction to detect and account for errors.

Error correction techniques involve encoding a logical qubit using multiple physical qubits. This introduces redundancy so that errors in a few physical qubits can be identified and corrected without affecting the logical qubit. However, existing error correction schemes require thousands of physical qubits per logical qubit due to the substantial overhead.

More efficient error correction would enable practical quantum computations using fewer physical resources. However, this requires fundamental advances in encoding and decoding algorithms, fault-tolerant logic gate design, and qubit connectivity.

Specialized Hardware Needs

Quantum computing places steep demands on computing hardware to enable qubit operations. Cryogenic systems for cooling to millikelvin temperatures are essential for superconducting qubits. However, expanding cryo-cooling infrastructure substantially is challenging today.

Laser, microwave, and magnetic control systems must also apply signals with precision down to picoseconds and nanometer scales to manipulate qubit states. This requires specialized electronic components and microfabrication processes that have yet to be widely available. Accessing such capabilities may necessitate partnerships with national labs.

Quantum computers promise enormous electricity processing to tackle complex problems like drug discovery, cryptography, and energy systems modeling. However, several technological hurdles must be overcome before constructing practical quantum computer systems.

The main challenge is that traditional qubits want to be cooled to just fractions above absolute zero with the use of steeply-priced refrigeration, costing thousands and thousands of greenbacks. This makes scaling up qubit numbers more challenging.

But researchers at UNSW Sydney, led by Professor Andrew Dzurak, have now demonstrated silicon-based qubits operating at 1.5 Kelvin. While still requiring cryogenic cooling, this is over 100 times warmer than conventional qubits. Silicon qubits leveraging existing semiconductor fabrication offer significant advantages. Less extreme cooling only needs affordable, compact refrigeration costing thousands instead of millions. This makes chips with larger qubit counts feasible.

Additionally, silicon qubits are compatible with classical computing chips controlling the quantum processor, unlike conventional qubits disrupted by ambient heat. Classical-quantum integration is essential for practical operation. This on-chip integration was proven using CMOS silicon electronics and qubits on the same prototype, a significant stepping stone.

Classical components can control qubit operation and readout without interference. The researchers designed a quantum architecture with qubits arranged in compact 3D structures. This maximizes qubit numbers per chip while minimizing wiring complexity. Commercial foundry processes can manufacture silicon qubit chips. While silicon qubits operate at higher temperatures than other types, they still achieve high-performance metrics like long coherence times. This indicates they have potential for error-corrected, fault-tolerant quantum computing. Moreover, silicon qubits build on the immense infrastructure and knowledge base for conventional silicon chip fabrication. This provides a rapid pathway to scale up compared to exotic qubit materials.UNSW also develops complementary technologies like quantum interconnects for on-chip qubit linking and quantum-ready CMOS electronics. Ongoing research aims to demonstrate a complete silicon-based quantum processor.

There are still challenges like improving qubit fidelities and developing practical error correction. But silicon qubit demonstrations represent major leaps in overcoming critical roadblocks toward realizable quantum computers.

With rapid advances, quantum computing power could be commercially available within years rather than decades. The teams' innovations bring this revolutionary technology much closer to practical implementation.

Limited Access to Quantum Computers

While cloud services are emerging to provide remote access to early quantum computers, availability remains sparse. Enterprises need more options to experiment with different quantum computing architectures matched to their specific use cases and algorithms.

Cross-compatible software is also lacking, often requiring customization to run optimally on different quantum hardware. More standards are needed to allow porting of code across platforms. Developing standard interfaces and benchmarks will help boost adoption as more commercial systems emerge.

Significant Talent Shortages

There is a tiny talent pool with multidisciplinary skills in physics, materials science, computer science, engineering, and mathematics required for quantum computing research and development. Building internal expertise or hiring specialists is exceedingly tricky currently.

Expanding university programs in quantum information science is critical to grow this specialized workforce. Partnerships with national labs and technology leaders would accelerate practical training. Upskilling existing staff through certifications and on-the-job training may also help fill talent gaps.

Implementation Planning Challenges

Quantum computing requires detailed strategic planning for enterprise adoption rather than isolated initiatives. Roadmaps are needed to identify target use cases while integrating with existing infrastructure across IT, R&D, and business teams.

Relevant technical and algorithmic skills must be cultivated before adoption. Legal and IP considerations around accessing external quantum services also need resolution. Furthermore, organizations must consider the potentially disruptive implications of quantum computing on business models, products, and markets.

Security Vulnerabilities

Quantum algorithms could break standard encryption schemes like RSA by efficiently factoring large primes. This allows later decryption of intercepted communications, threatening data security. Post-quantum cryptography is needed to enable secure data transmission and storage.

Quantum key distribution via quantum channels offers inherent security, but dedicated infrastructure is required. Additionally, quantum machine learning could help generate malicious online content, demanding mitigation. Overall, cybersecurity strategies should incorporate quantum threat monitoring.

Significant Technical Investment Needed

The considerable costs of building internal quantum computing capabilities or accessing cloud-based services may deter adoption. However, fees may fall as technologies mature over time. Strategic partnerships can provide early access to capabilities. Government programs also help fund research infrastructure. Overall, before resource allocation, careful analysis of return on investment and mission impact is required.

Ongoing Research Efforts and Advances

While profound challenges exist, rapid progress in quantum research provides optimism. Government and industry labs are demonstrating new performance milestones frequently.

Novel materials like topological insulators or nanowire networks overcome qubit issues. Architectures using modularly extensible qubit arrays tackle scalability. Growing collaborations between academia, national labs, and tech firms should accelerate advances through knowledge sharing. Sustained investments and commercialization efforts will unlock quantum capabilities for real-world problems.

Hardware and Materials

Mastering qubit decoherence remains a pivotal hardware challenge. Environmental disturbances can cause qubits to lose their delicate quantum states, leading to errors. This demands advances in materials science and nanofabrication methods to isolate better and protect qubits. Developing quantum error correction techniques is another vital need to detect and fix errors during computation.

Scaling up the number of qubits also poses immense difficulties. Expanding to the hundreds or thousands of qubits needed for practical applications while maintaining low error rates is challenging. This requires optimizing qubit design, control electronics, interconnects, and system architecture. Each qubit technology, such as superconducting loops, trapped ions, or quantum dots, has unique strengths and weaknesses that must be balanced in a system.

Software and System Integration

Software tools tailored for quantum programming remain at nascent stages. Quantum algorithms have complex requirements compared to classical code, necessitating new programming languages, compilers, simulators, and debugging tools. Hybrid algorithms spanning classical and quantum processors need seamless integration to leverage their complementary capabilities.

The need for standards and benchmarks for evaluating software and hardware hinders progress. Developing these would aid wider adoption across platforms. Optimizing interfaces for transferring data between quantum and classical systems poses engineering challenges, too.

Talent Development and Training

Another challenge is that There is also a significant shortage of skilled quantum engineers, programmers, and researchers. Multidisciplinary understanding spanning physics, materials technology, electronics, computer science, and mathematics is the expertise required. Expanding the quantum-ready workforce demands substantial investments in education and training programs at academic institutions and industry collaborations.

Expenses and Funding

The considerable costs of specialized quantum hardware and facilities and attracting talent make quantum computing highly expensive. Significant funding for both research and commercialization is essential for progress. While government agencies currently provide significant investments, developing self-sustaining commercial models would be beneficial over the long term.

Grounds for Optimism

Despite the challenges, rapid advances in quantum research and engineering provide optimism. Hardware demonstrations regularly achieve new performance milestones, showing steady improvements in qubit numbers, fidelity, and control. Innovations in materials, cryogenics, electronics, and laser technology are overcoming barriers. Growing commercialization efforts will drive more applications-focused R&D. Expanding collaborations between academia, national labs, and industry should accelerate progress through knowledge sharing. With concerted strategic actions, the UAE can cultivate expertise to become a leader in this emerging field.

Quantum Thinking in Problem Solving

Addressing multifaceted roadblocks requires a creative approach that leverages the UAE's unique Quantum Management model. Quantum thinking applied to governance and policymaking fosters decentralized, innovative solutions to meet emerging challenges.

The nation has already employed quantum-inspired strategies effectively in many domains. For instance, the Mohammed bin Rashid Space Centre dynamically advances space research by swiftly prototyping rockets and satellites. The UAE's response to COVID-19 utilized a tech-driven Quantum curve-flattening model, striking a balance between health and economic priorities. Similarly, Dubai's Museum of the Future combines future foresight and design thinking to prototype innovative policy solutions. Government bodies like the Emirates Scientists Council, Emirates Foundation for Schools Education, and the Federal Youth Authority exemplify the decentralized, grassroots approach to innovation and human capital development that characterizes Quantum governance.

Such initiatives highlight the power of decentralized governance, public-private collaboration, and future-focused vision in addressing complex challenges. As the nation progresses toward its goals, amplifying and expanding the application of Quantum thinking will be vital.

Economic Challenges and Quantum Adaptations

Navigating economic uncertainties and energy transitions towards 2050 is daunting. Yet, the UAE tackles this by diversifying its economy and embracing Quantum Economics, offering adaptive strategies for resilience. Persisting oil price fluctuations emphasize the importance of expanding non-oil sectors. Accelerating growth in technology, logistics, tourism, and renewables becomes imperative. Policies like expanding Golden Visas, boosting foreign investment, and enabling start-up ecosystems will strengthen economic diversification. Training citizens in future skills like coding and amplifying the contributions of women in the workforce also bolsters resilience.

Fiscal policies aligned with Quantum Economics shore up stability. Increased efficiency in government spending, stronger public-private partnerships, and agile SME support optimize resource allocation. The digitalization of economic sectors results in faster, more agile policy responses. The application of behavioral economics provides insights into consumer behavior patterns.

Quantum Finance tools like AI-driven stock market monitoring help moderate market fluctuations. Blockchain integration increases banking transparency and cross-border financial flows. Adopting cryptocurrency regulation fosters the measured development of this emerging asset class. The UAE's economic policy ecosystem integrates foresight and agility to address evolving challenges.

Technological Hurdles and Quantum Innovations

Staying ahead in the ever-evolving tech landscape is vital for the UAE's competitive edge. Quantum leaps in computing, AI, nanotech, and beyond can surmount challenges, fueling the nation's innovation ecosystem. Enhancing cybersecurity and data governance is a key priority. Initiatives like the Emirates Blockchain Strategy foster secure digital infrastructure. Regulations around data privacy, technology ethics, and autonomous vehicles align innovation with the public interest—investments in quantum encryption and AI-enabled defense boost cyber-resilience.

Cutting-edge innovations spur progress in vital sectors. Dubai's self-driving transport strategy leverages intelligent traffic systems. Quantum AI enables personalized education and healthcare solutions. Technology hubs like Masdar City and Dubai Science Park drive R&D.

Policy sandboxing allows controlled testing of new technologies, as seen in the Dubai Future Accelerators program.

Futurist frameworks like the Museum of the Future prototype desired tech-societal futures. The UAE Artificial Intelligence Council steers national AI implementation. Multi Stakeholder digital governance is bolstered through bodies like the Dubai Future Councils. Overall, the UAE strategically channels quantum-guided technological advances to overcome roadblocks.

Societal and Cultural Shifts: Quantum Social Adaptations

Evolving socio cultural trends driven by technological change, demographic shifts, and globalization also pose governance challenges. Here, too, proactive policies rooted in Quantum principles help manage change. Promoting social cohesion is crucial in the UAE's cosmopolitan environment. Fostering interfaith and cross-cultural dialog through the Ministry of Tolerance and EXPO events creates inclusivity. Population centers like Abu Dhabi's Ghadan 21 district spur community engagement through urban planning. Gender balance initiatives also foster cohesive growth.

Improving livability and happiness is also vital. Practical schemes like Dubai's retiree residency visas, elderly care initiatives, and new insurance schemes respond to demographic needs— female empowerment efforts close the gender gap through support mechanisms, specialized funds, and equality-focused leadership programs. Creative architecture adds an aesthetic dimension to cityscapes.

Preserving cultural heritage while allowing space for organic evolution will be necessary— digital museums like Al Ain's Zayed National Museum leverage technology for cultural archiving. Contemporary cultural projects like Abu Dhabi's hip-hop scene and Dubai's art festivals encourage youth participation. The UAE deploys Quantum-aligned sociocultural strategies to keep pace with shifting trends.

Geopolitical Dynamics and Quantum Diplomacy

Navigating global realignments and geopolitical flux will require the UAE to employ its strategic Quantum Diplomacy model. Shifting relations between major powers, conflicts, and economic uncertainties in neighboring regions pose external challenges. However, the UAE is well-poised to leverage its influence as a peace broker and global hub. Ongoing tensions with Iran have been managed through pragmatism and de-escalation. The Abraham Accords reflect the potential for Quantum Diplomacy to reshape regional alignments. The UAE's stabilization efforts in Yemen demonstrate responsible crisis management under complex conditions.

Globally, the UAE continues serving as a connector between civilizations. Its humanitarian outreach, space diplomacy, and economic partnerships forge global collaboration. As a technologically advanced, socially progressive Muslim country, it is a model for the developing world. By proactively shaping global agendas like climate action, gender balance, and tolerance agency , the UAE exercises outsized soft power. The UAE deploys Quantum Diplomacy foresight fully to navigate geopolitical uncertainties, serving as a bridge-builder and pioneering change.

Adaptive Leadership in Times of Crisis

Navigating unforeseen crisis requires visionary yet agile leadership enabled by Quantum governance frameworks. The UAE's effective pandemic response reflected such adaptive leadership in action. Despite the health crisis, economic stimuli and pragmatic policies ensured continuity, earning global praise.

More broadly, the nation's technological and economic progress is made possible by proactive political leadership. Long-term plans like the UAE Vision 2050 and Dubai 2040 Urban Master Plan lay strategic foundations. However, their implementation is guided by regular reassessment of evolving ground realities.

High-level councils continuously align policies to changing priorities. Leaders like HH Sheikh Mohammed bin Rashid epitomize agile governance, rapidly responding to citizen feedback on social media. Knowledge exchange is enabled between the government and private sector through collaboration platforms like the World Government Summit.

Leadership development programs, including the Mohamed Bin Zayed University for Humanities, groom the next generation of dynamic Emirati leaders and entrepreneurs. Leadership roles for women are expanded through initiatives like the Gender Balance Council. Adaptive and visionary leadership underpins the UAE's agility in responding to emerging challenges.

Learning from Challenges: Quantum Resilience

The UAE has demonstrated fantastic resilience in the face of oil shocks, monetary crises, and geopolitical tensions. Proactively gaining knowledge of these demanding situations has continuously evolved and bolstered its governance model.

Periodic stresses and crises provide opportunities for self-appraisal and course correction. For instance, the 2008 financial crash triggered several economic reforms and stimulus policies. The 2011 Arab Spring led to a greater focus on youth empowerment and happiness policies. The pandemic accelerated digitalization across sectors.

Policy experiments like Dubai's solar energy park and electric vehicle infrastructure catalyze more innovative long-term strategies. Pilot projects provide empirical learning. Global best practices are adapted to local contexts. Course correction is enabled by high-frequency policy feedback loops leveraging big data analytics.

The recursive process of learning from challenges has honed the UAE's governance capacities. The nation has developed institutional resilience ingrained with Quantum thinking by continually stress-testing its systems. This positions it well to handle unforeseen crises and leverage challenges as opportunities.

Vision 2050: Quantum-Driven Solutions

The UAE's ahead-searching governance architecture is laying the principles to address the coming years' demanding situations. Vision 2050 envisions lengthy-term techniques across all sectors powered by technological innovation and human capital development.

Emerging sectors like renewables, fintech, and biotech will see a massive enlargement, enabled by investments in R&D and destiny skills applications. Stakeholder capitalism will strengthen economic resilience, guided by the principles of Quantum Economics. Hyperloop transport and AI healthcare signal ambitious technological goals. Cultural and quality-of-life indices will complement financial metrics.

The realization of Vision 2050 will be enabled by agile policymaking and continuous ecosystem support. Policies will stay ahead of emerging socio-economic shifts, aided by foresight bodies like the Museum of the Future. Lifelong learning and skills retraining will smooth workforce transitions. Digital governance and predictive analytics will help data-driven decision-making.

The UAE is primed to be pioneering in spearheading quantum technological advances. Its prototype quantum computer and quantum research centers anchor cutting-edge R&D. Quantum encryption and desalination exemplify potential applications. Investments in quantum education create ripple effects. Overall, the UAE is harnessing quantum advances to power its future.

In summary, the UAE charts its course to 2050, anticipating new challenges is inevitable. Yet, with a governance model grounded in Quantum Management standards, it gains the agility and resilience to navigate diverse obstacles. It has developed institutional readiness to handle complex uncertainties by stress testing its systems. Quantum thinking applied across policy domains fosters decentralized and creative solutions. A strategic vision guided by foresight lays the groundwork for long-term ambitions. Pragmatic and adaptive leadership steers realizing national goals, leveraging collaborative networks. Technology is harnessed to accelerate human progress. This unique governance approach positions the UAE well to overcome future roadblocks and realize its Vision 2050 aspirations. The nation's journey continues to highlight the pivotal role of Quantum Management in building a competitive knowledge economy and pioneering the future.

CHAPTER 13

QUANTUM AGRICULTURE
AND FOOD SECURITY

In a world where population growth and climate change are principal problems, agriculture is one of the critical pillars of human civilization. The UAE is aware of the significance of this enterprise and has made significant monetary outlays to boost meal safety via state-of-the-art technology. But what if there was a way to take this innovation further? There is now a revolutionary new approach, Quantum Management. With these adaptability, decentralization, and futurity principles, the UAE can trailblaze a transformation that will redefine farming. Once cutting-edge quantum technologies like artificial intelligence, Internet of Things sensors, and satellite systems are integrated into the system, possibilities for optimizing crop yields as well as resource utilization become limitless. In terms of sustainability, less is more. Moreover, quantum-inspired techniques can also be a decisive factor in reducing waste and increasing resilience when faced with environmental stresses.

With the UAE now embarking on Vision 2050, which is splitting off with a project designed to ensure national food safety and become an early achiever in new technologies, Quantum Agriculture becomes a beacon of hope. The UAE can be one of the global pioneers in this strategic field by taking the initiative to establish an innovative and sustainable agricultural ecosystem. In this era of rapid change, when the future environment for our planet is still uncertain, Quantum Agriculture offers a brighter and more certain future.

In this chapter, we'll explore the exciting field of Quantum Agriculture and its effect on food supply. In addition, we will learn about the use of quantum technologies to improve agricultural efficiency and how new farming techniques inspired by quantum can guarantee food security. The possibility of an agri-food revolution combining precision with high levels of sustainability also becomes apparent from this vantage point.

Applying Quantum Technologies to Enhance Agricultural Efficiency

The agricultural applications of quantum technologies have recently drawn attention. These advanced technologies promise to improve farming processes and increase productivity in sustainable resource utilization. Farmers and agricultural enterprises can innovate on precision farming, crop monitoring, and resource utilization using such quantum-inspired methods. Higher efficiency, and better food security will result.

Precision Farming:

In precision farming, all the various cultivation operations are carried out using precision and accuracy. Gathering and analyzing large amounts of data are the tasks for which quantum technologies are best suited. Temp, humidity, and soil composition are analyzed using quantum AI and machine learning techniques to optimize irrigation, fertilizer use, and harvesting. This data-driven approach uses resources efficiently, avoids waste, and increases yield.

For example, the Al Khazanah Quantum Farm in Abu Dhabi uses sensory systems based on quantum computing. With networked quantum sensors and novel AI, the farm optimizes crop yield, particularly tomatoes and cucumbers. Water consumption is minimized as a result of this process. These sensors detect the many environmental factors, returning real-time data to an AI system that decides how much water and fertilizer is applied. This ensures ideal growing conditions for fauna.

Crop Monitoring:

With quantum technologies, achieving levels of monitoring crop growth and health that have never been seen will be possible. When coupled with IoT devices, quantum sensor networks monitor crop growth and field soil conditions. Farmers can measure such parameters as soil moisture and plant nutrients with these sensors. Farmers can proactively approach pest control and disease prevention with this information and manage their crops overall.

One example is using drones with quantum sensors and cameras to monitor crops. The drones can take high-definition photos of produce. Farmers then use the images to detect potential headaches, such as nutrient deficiencies or insect outbreaks. This data ensures that farmers can act quickly and precisely to minimize risk and promote crop health.

Resource Utilization:

Sustainable agriculture requires efficient resource utilization. Quantum technologies provide novel ways to maximize the utilization of resources--including water, energy, and fertilizer. Farmers can reduce waste and their environmental impact by precisely measuring and managing the use of resources.

Systems based on quantum inspiration, like those built in the Emirates Soilless Agriculture Innovation Centre, are indispensable to automated control. Such systems combine Hydroponics with renewable energy sources and sophisticated monitoring technologies to create sustainable farm crops. Guided by this quantum-driven automation, the Centre conserves resources and creates optimum environmental conditions for plant growth.

For example Farms and agricultural enterprises worldwide have already brought in quantum technologies to increase farming efficiency. For instance, Quantum Inspire is being used inside the Netherlands to expand quantum algorithms for optimizing greenhouse weather manipulation. Using the electricity of quantum computing, farmers can alter environmental elements like temperature, humidity, and CO2 levels to create ideal conditions for their plants. Moreover, in Australia, a Quantum Computing for Agriculture project hopes to use quantum technologies to optimize farm management decision-making. Quantum algorithms can analyze large datasets to provide crop performance forecasts, weather patterns, and market trends, which will help growers plan planting times, harvest dates, and market strategies.

Thus, the involvement of quantum technologies in agriculture promises enormous potential to raise efficiency and productivity. The impact of quantum-inspired solutions has already been marked in areas such as precision farming, crop monitoring, and resource utilization. The successful integration of quantum technologies into agricultural practice is illustrated by real-life examples: the Al Khazanah Quantum Farm and the Quantum Inspire platform. In our quest to exploit and develop quantum technologies, agriculture's future looks bright as yields increase, waste decreases, and food security practices are strengthened.

Securing Food Through Quantum-style Farming Methods

With the population still increasing, food security is an international concern. Agricultural methods inspired by quantum science provide new ideas to meet this challenge by optimizing farming practices and food production.

These quantum-inspired computing solutions have the power to transform crop cultivation and resource use. Based on quantum algorithms, farmers can use large amounts of data to make well-informed choices concerning irrigation, fertilization, and pest control. Using such methods, it is possible to perform precise and focused actions that minimize excessive use of resources while maximizing yield.

Quantum-inspired farming has precision agriculture as an essential part. Combined with quantum sensors and mobile devices, farmers can monitor crops in real-time. Knowing this, interventions can be done in time to change irrigation schedules or apply fertilizer only where needed. To reduce waste and raise overall efficiency, farmers can optimize resource use.

Autonomous farming systems also benefit from quantum-inspired techniques. Quantum A.I.-driven robots can remove weeds and hunt down pests with laser-like accuracy. In this way, farmers are ensured good crop management by outsourcing these labor-intensive jobs to machines.

Precision and sustainability: Revolutionizing the Agri-Food Industry.

The pressure for sustainability and efficiency in agriculture has necessitated a transformation of the agri-food industry. This industry needs revolution, and quantum-inspired farming techniques provide just the amount of routine.

Another idea inspiring farmers is a quantum-inspired technique called Hydroponics, which uses nutrient-rich water instead of traditional soil. Hydroponic systems use quantum principles to save water and energy, reduce land requirements, and grow crops under controlled conditions. They allow year-round production, regardless of the weather, and can also be employed in town. These factors facilitate local foodstuffs.

Another aspect of quantum-inspired farming is the integration of renewable energy. Farmers can lower their carbon footprint while practicing sustainable agriculture by harnessing the power of renewable energy sources such as solar. Systems modeled on quantum physics also help control energy use so that renewable resources can be fully utilized.

QI-inspired methods can make a big difference in another area where blockchain technology is being applied, the agri-food industry. With blockchain, there is a safe and open environment to trace the source of food products and their genuineness. Quantum encryption adds another level to data security to secure necessary information.

In a nutshell, quantum-infused farming techniques have the potential to elevate agricultural efficiency and improve food supply stability while also promoting revolution in agri-food industries. Using quantum technologies, including AI and IoT sensors, and satellite systems for crop yield optimization means minimizing waste and promoting sustainability. With projects like the Emirates Soilless Agriculture Innovation Centre, the UAE is at least leading in adopting these methods and promoting agricultural innovation. As advancements and investments continue, quantum agriculture is breaking new ground by working to create an innovative, eco-friendly food ecosystem for tomorrow.

Optimized Farming Harnesses Quantum Sensing

Advanced quantum sensors enable real-time measurement of soil conditions, crop growth parameters, and other variables for data-driven precision agriculture. Quantum computing also facilitates complex predictive climate and weather modeling for proactive disaster management.

Quantum gravimetry leverages free-falling atoms and interferometry to accurately map subsurface features like soil composition, terrain contours, and water tables. This provides invaluable data on variability across farms to target interventions. Quantum sensors like trapped ions are ideal for detecting electric fields and could monitor plant health and moisture stresses.

Hyperspectral imaging from quantum satellites can assess crop growth across vast areas. Overall, the combination of quantum sensing and computing provides invaluable real-time data for optimizing decisions in precision agriculture, boosting productivity, incomes, and sustainability.

The UAE's focus on enhancing domestic food security and its track record of rapidly adopting advanced technologies position it to lead in quantum sensing applications. Precision optimization of scarce resources like water will be crucial in its arid climate. Targeted investments into quantum research partnerships, pilot projects, and commercialization efforts will catalyze innovation.

Harnessing Quantum Computing to Advance Agriculture

Quantum computing promises to transform agriculture by enabling rapid analysis of vast datasets around genetics, climate, and other multivariate factors affecting crop yields and farming economics. Conventional computers need help to simultaneously process so many complex, dynamically interacting variables.

But quantum computers are ideal for such optimization problems. Their exponential scale-up allows the modeling of complex cropping systems and genetics. This can help derive optimal adaptive strategies for precision agriculture based on soil, weather, and crop data to maximize yields. Quantum simulation can also accelerate targeted breeding for desired traits like drought resistance.

However, adoption faces challenges like high costs of early quantum systems and cultural resistance among traditional farmers. Initial quantum-classical hybrid cloud systems may enable a smooth transition by augmenting existing analytics. Overall, quantum computing could drive step-change advances in agriculture to improve food security globally.

The UAE's Quantum Management approach, which integrates the latest technologies with human factors, provides a model to address adoption barriers. Its investments in quantum research centers and global partnerships also lay the groundwork to harness quantum agriculture.

Unlocking the Potential of Quantum Computing for Agriculture

Quantum computing represents a potential breakthrough technology to help improve food security and agricultural resilience. Conventional computing uses binary bits, but quantum computing utilizes 'qubits' to represent multiple states simultaneously. This enables exponential scaling in processing power.

While today's computers struggle to analyze highly complex systems like plant genetics, quantum computers are well-suited to such tasks. There are countless possible genetic combinations determining traits like drought resistance in crops. Testing them through selective breeding and trials takes years.

But quantum computers could model plant genomes and directly identify optimal gene combinations for desired traits like higher yields or climate resilience. This would dramatically accelerate the development of improved crop varieties.

Robust quantum simulation of plant genetics could also reveal insights beyond current knowledge. It may enable determining theoretical maximum yields possible for a crop under certain conditions, transcending incremental improvements. Genome editing tools like CRISPR could rapidly modify crops to manifest the computationally derived gene combinations. This could create resilient new varieties in months rather than decades.

However, fully developed quantum computers are still years away. But near-term hybrid systems combining quantum and classical computing could already achieve significant leaps in agricultural modeling capabilities. Quantum advances could unlock an unprecedented understanding of plant genetics and traits. This can arm plant breeders with new tools to accelerate the development of resilient, highly productive crops. Quantum-enabled agriculture promises to be a pivotal technology in ensuring future food security. The UAE's investments in quantum computing research and partnerships put it in a solid position to lead quantum applications in agriculture. As a global hub focused on food security, the nation can bridge quantum capabilities with farming needs to pioneer resilient Crop variety.

Revolutionizing the Agri-Food Industry with Precision and Sustainability

The agri-food industry is crucial in ensuring food protection and the developing demand for sustainable and nutritious meals. By embracing Quantum Management practices, the world can revolutionize its operations to improve efficiency, sustainability, and overall food security.

Enhancing Supply Chain Optimization and Logistics

Quantum technology provides exceptional potential in optimizing delivery chain operations, lowering wastage, and enhancing logistics. Quantum-inspired algorithms enable extra correct calls for forecasting, allowing outlets to control stock and minimize overstocking or understocking. This, now not the most effective, reduces meal waste; however, it additionally ensures a steady delivery of sparkling produce to customers.

Additionally, quantum sensors and IoT devices can reveal bloodless garage centers in real-time, ensuring the most effective temperature and humidity conditions to limit spoilage. These advancements in logistics and delivery chain control decorate the general efficiency of the agri-food supply.

Promoting Sustainable Practices in Agriculture

Quantum-driven answers have the potential to revolutionize agricultural practices, making them extra sustainable and environmentally friendly. Quantum precision agriculture, for example, utilizes drones ready with superior sensors to accumulate data on soil moisture, nutrient degrees, and crop fitness. This fact is then analyzed by the use of quantum AI algorithms to optimize irrigation schedules and nutrient software, lowering water usage and minimizing the environmental impact of farming.

Furthermore, the quantum blockchain era can decorate traceability inside the agri-food supply chain. By leveraging the immutability and transparency of blockchain, customers can, without difficulty, trace the origins of their food, ensuring meal protection and promoting ethical and sustainable farming practices.

Showcasing Quantum-Driven Transformation in Agri-Food

The United Arab Emirates (UAE) has been at the vanguard of embracing quantum technologies to convert the agri-food enterprise. The kingdom's food protection approach encompasses numerous projects, including studies and improvement, infrastructure development, and international partnerships, all guided by the aid of quantum wandering.

One incredible venture is the Silal Food Technology Hub in Abu Dhabi. This innovation hub offers modern-day infrastructure and know-how to meal organizations, encouraging the adoption of quantum-stimulated practices. By facilitating collaboration between farmers, food processors, and outlets, Silal Hub speeds up the development and implementation of sustainable and efficient procedures throughout the agri-food cost chain.

The UAE's dedication to food protection and quantum-driven agriculture is further verified through initiatives like the Emirates Soilless Agriculture Innovation Centre. This center promotes the usage of Hydroponics and other quantum-inspired strategies to obtain sustainable farming practices in arid environments.

Hence, the agri-food industry faces several challenges, including the need for elevated efficiency, sustainability, and food safety. Quantum technology provides an effective toolset to deal with those challenges head-on. From optimizing delivery chain operations to promoting sustainable farming practices, the agri-food industry can leverage quantum management ideas to revolutionize its approaches and ensure a brighter and more stable destiny for food production.

By embracing Quantum Management practices, the enterprise can harness the electricity of quantum technologies to achieve precision, sustainability, and steady meals for all in the long run. The UAE's pioneering efforts in this field function as a testament to the transformative capability of quantum-stimulated solutions inside the agri-food quarter.

Challenges in Implementing Quantum Agriculture

While quantum technology promises significant benefits, effectively integrating it into real-world agriculture poses challenges. Initial deployment costs, training requirements, and cultural resistance are common hurdles. A quantum mindset emphasizes adaptability and continuous improvement to overcome such barriers.

For instance, farmers may be reluctant to adopt new technologies, needing more hands-on demonstration and training. Conducting controlled pilot projects at innovation farms allows for showcasing benefits more concretely, inspiring wider adoption. Similarly, concerns around data privacy need to be addressed upfront through robust security protocols and education.

As technologies evolve, policies and training programs need continuous updating to align human capabilities with automation. Investments in both physical and human capital are essential for long-term success. For example, the UAE provides agricultural scholarships and vocational programs to build required skill sets across generations.

The Emirates Soilless Agriculture Innovation Centre also frequently upgrades technologies based on the latest research to accelerate development. Overall, iterative experiments, stakeholder engagement, and adaptive policies help smoothly integrate quantum agriculture.

Overcoming Challenges for Mainstream

While promising significant benefits, quantum technologies face adoption hurdles like high costs, cultural resistance, and lack of technical expertise. However, tailored strategies can promote mainstream usage of quantum-enabled solutions.

Targeted incentive policies, subsidies, and loans can help farmers transition by easing costs. Extensive demonstration projects at digital innovation farms allow for showcasing benefits to inspire voluntary uptake. Educational initiatives are vital to developing talent pipelines and quantum-ready workforces across agriculture. Updating policies, regulations, and technologies continuously based on user feedback will also smooth adoption.

The UAE's experience with challenges in emerging technologies provides lessons applicable to quantum agriculture. Its continuous emphasis on fostering specialized skills and expertise locally and through global talent acquisition is a crucial enabler. Such efforts will lay the groundwork for successfully harnessing quantum agriculture.

Vision 2050: Quantum-Enabled Agricultural Future

The Vision 2050 initiative in the UAE sets bold goals for the future of agriculture, leveraging quantum technologies to ensure sustainable and steady meal manufacturing. This lengthy-term vision encompasses the combination of quantum-stimulated innovations in farming practices and meal manufacturing structures, paving the way for a quantum-enabled agricultural future.

1. Quantum-Driven Innovations in Farming and Food Production

Quantum Agriculture will revolutionize farming practices, aid control, and food manufacturing systems. By harnessing the energy of quantum technology, farmers can optimize crop growth, improve helpful resource usage, and decorate standard efficiency. Quantum sensors and AI algorithms will offer real-time information on soil conditions, crop fitness, and environmental factors, permitting farmers to make specific selections concerning irrigation, fertilization, and pest management. This records-driven technique will maximize crop yields while minimizing environmental impact.

2. Sustainable and Secure Food Ecosystems

Quantum technology will be vital in establishing sustainable and stable food ecosystems in the UAE. By leveraging quantum computing, farms can optimize electricity intake and reduce waste through advanced automation and clever energy management systems. Additionally, quantum-inspired improvements in indoor farming, vertical agriculture, and Hydroponics will enable 12 months of spherical crop production, reducing the reliance on conventional farming methods and mitigating the impact of climate alternatives on meal manufacturing.

3. Quantum-Driven Pilot Projects and R&D Centers

The UAE's dedication to quantum-enabled agriculture is evident through the establishment of pilot projects and research centers devoted to exploring the capacity of quantum technology in the agricultural quarter. These tasks function as testbeds for quantum-inspired farming strategies, vertical farms powered by renewable electricity, computerized hydroponic systems, and precision irrigation. The records and insights from these tasks will inform future techniques and rules for the sizable adoption of Quantum Agriculture.

4. Quantum Education and Collaboration

Vision 2050 recognizes the importance of building a skilled staff able to harness the potential of quantum technology in agriculture. Workforce skilling projects will identify supplying farmers, meal specialists, and agri-commercial enterprise leaders with the necessary know-how and competencies to enforce quantum-driven solutions. Furthermore, collaborations with international partners in studies and development will foster innovation and boost the commercialization of quantum technology in the agri-meals zone.

Therefore, Vision 2050 sets forth an ambitious roadmap for mixing quantum technologies into the rural quarter within the UAE. Quantum Agriculture will force sustainable practices, enhance meal safety, and pave the way for a future where farming is optimized through information-driven choice-making and progressive strategies. By embracing quantum-stimulated improvements, the UAE is poised to become a global chief in sustainable and secure meal ecosystems, ensuring a prosperous destiny for future generations.

Now, let's flow toward the end of this bankruptcy. In the massive expanse of agriculture, where the success of countries is based on their ability to feed their populations, Quantum Management emerges as a recreation-changer for the UAE. With their substantial capacity, quantum technologies maintain the importance of unlocking remarkable possibilities for enhancing productiveness, performance, sustainability, and, in the end, meal safety. Imagine a destiny in which quantum-powered AI algorithms examine widespread information to optimize each aspect of farming operations. From precision planting to sensible irrigation structures, that technology will revolutionize how we develop our meals. Quantum-stimulated strategies will reduce wastage and decrease agriculture's environmental impact, ensuring a healthier planet for future generations.

But attaining this vision calls for more than simply technological advancements. It needs strategic investments in studies, sturdy infrastructure, and professional workforce development. By nurturing a quantum-literate era, the UAE can boost the tempo of innovation in agriculture, leading the way closer to a greater sustainable and secure destiny. By harnessing the strength of Quantum Management, the UAE will no longer ensure its meals are safe but also inspire different nations to embody the transformative capability of quantum-driven agriculture.

CHAPTER 14

QUANTUM EXPLORATION OF THE OCEANS

Do you know that Oceans cover over 70% of Earth's surface and contain 97% of the planet's water? They are home to diverse marine life and provide food for billions. Yet there is still much we must discover in the seas' depths. In recent years, the United Arab Emirates (UAE) has emerged as a leader in applying advanced technologies like quantum computing and artificial intelligence to ocean exploration and marine research. The country is pioneering quantum physics and science to transform how people connect with the oceans. The UAE's ambitious vision leverages quantum technologies to study ocean life and natural resources in unprecedented detail, overcoming the limitations of conventional oceanography. The UAE is committed to developing a sustainable blue economy, promoting innovative and ecologically sound ideas to grow prosperity while safeguarding nature. Understanding the oceans will be critical as the UAE charts its Journey to 2050 to become a foremost global player in adopting high-tech, sustainable solutions. This initiative aims to demonstrate how quantum science can transform marine studies and ocean stewardship, enabling the UAE to develop a thriving ocean economy by 2050 that sustains people and the planet.

This chapter looks at how quantum science is changing how people relate to oceans - from using special machines for deep-sea discovery to based on it. Going further into marine study is inspired by what happens in a world where everything's tiny, like atoms (we call this "quantum"). It shows how the UAE is leading in using quantum tech to learn and protect ocean life.

Using Quantum Sensors for Underwater Explorations in the Deep Sea

A place where quantum science is helping explore and study oceans a lot is by making very accurate quantum sensors. Traditional sensors face inherent limitations in accuracy and precision, especially in deep subsea environments under extreme pressures and temperatures. Quantum sensors leverage unique quantum effects like entanglement, superposition, and squeezing to achieve unprecedented sensitivity and measurement precision.

For example, quantum gravimeters utilizing matter wave interferometry of Bose-Einstein condensates can detect underwater minuscule fluctuations in gravitational fields. This grants researchers new abilities to map detailed ocean floor contours, identify lucrative offshore oil and gas reservoirs, see hydrothermal vents and subsea volcanoes, and find ancient shipwrecks and submerged artifacts with far greater precision than ever achievable.

The Ocean Gravity Exploration Survey System developed by Lockheed Martin utilizes quantum gravimeters to chart seafloor gravity accurately. Surveys offshore New Zealand have discovered previously unmapped seabed features and guided offshore drilling operations.

Quantum gyroscopes exploiting quantum superposition also outperform classical gyroscopes limited by thermal noise. On marine research vessels, quantum gyroscopes enable exact turning maneuvers, acceleration measurements, and dynamic positioning even in rough seas. This enormously benefits tasks like underwater surveys, oilfield discovery, and retrieval of subsea resources.

For example, the BQ1 quantum gyroscope developed by Honeywell enables accurate heading measurements on ships even in turbulent Arctic conditions. Meanwhile, quantum magnetometers utilizing quantum coherence effects are up to a hundred times more sensitive than traditional counterparts in precisely measuring magnetic fields. This is immensely useful in pinpointing hydrothermal vent activity and magnetically anomalous seabed features.

The UAE is pioneering quantum sensor research and development through efforts at institutions like the Quantum Research Lab at Khalifa University. Researchers there are actively developing next-generation quantum gravimeters, magnetometers, and gyroscopes targeted explicitly for commercial, defence, and scientific maritime applications. With precise real-time positioning and orientation data, UAE researchers envision advanced autonomous underwater drones surveying the seas guided by quantum-enhanced inertial navigation systems.

Quantum sensing grants remarkable and transformative insights into marine geophysics, chemistry, and biology once hidden from view. As quantum technologies mature, deeper and more illuminating exploration of the oceans will become increasingly feasible worldwide. The UAE is positioned at the global forefront of this question. Apologies for the previous response.

Revolutionizing Oceanography with Quantum Sensors

The creation of quantum sensors is changing the study of oceanography by letting us measure the marine world in new ways. These measurements are super-accurate and sensitive like never before. These new quantum machines use extraordinary things from the science of tiny particles, like entanglement and superposition. They help fix problems that old ocean sensors can't solve.

One primary application uses quantum gravimeters, magnetometers, and gyroscopes to map the seafloor with extraordinary precision. The quantum sensors can pinpoint minute variations in gravity, magnetism, and orientation to chart seafloor features, identify hydrothermal vents, locate shipwrecks, and detect underwater volcanoes or subsea oil and gas reservoirs. This grants remarkable new insights into the geology and resources of the seafloor that were previously hidden.

Another critical use is tracking climate change through ultra-sensitive monitoring of ocean conditions. Quantum sensors detect tiny temperature changes, sea level rise, current variations, and salinity shifts. This helps scientists better understand climate impacts and improve predictive models. Quantum radar technology also enables tracking cyclones and storms offshore with greater accuracy.

Quantum sensors deployed on research vessels empower new abilities for ocean mapping and surveys via precise navigation, even in rough seas. The remarkable stability and sensitivity of quantum gyroscopes facilitate maneuvers and dynamic positioning when exploring remote or turbulent waters.

Quantum sensing has genuinely revolutionary implications for oceanography and marine science across domains. These futuristic devices open new windows into the mysteries of the deep oceans and seafloor that hold many valuable resources and secrets yet to be discovered. The UAE is pioneering the adoption of quantum technology in ocean applications through trailblazing research projects. Quantum sensing marks the next frontier in advancing humanity's knowledge of the invaluable marine environment.

Quantum-Inspired Marine Biology Research and Conservation Efforts

Beyond novel sensors, the foundational principles of quantum physics inspire innovative approaches to marine biology research and conservation. Concepts like entanglement, superposition, quantum coherence, and parallelism offer radically new perspectives for understanding the function of marine ecosystems and organisms.

Quantum Navigation in Marine Animals

One fascinating area of research is exploring how marine animals utilize quantum phenomena for navigation and migration. Certain species, such as sea turtles, birds, and lobsters, are believed to rely on Earth's natural magnetic field for long-distance movement. Quantum behaviors may play a role in these processes. Scientists are actively investigating magnetically sensitive chemical reactions in these species, searching for potential quantum biology foundations. By studying the quantum properties, researchers aim to uncover the mechanisms that allow these animals to navigate vast distances.

Quantum Coherence in Marine Phytoplankton

Marine plant life called phytoplankton is being researched for a fascinating quantum thing called coherence. These tiny living things are essential in the sea. They do something called photosynthesis and help make food for other ocean creatures. Scientists are looking into how quantum coherence helps make photosynthesis more efficient in ocean plants called phytoplankton. Understanding the tiny things in this process could help us use energy better for fake plant systems. This might be used to make cleaner power methods someday.

Taking a quantum lens to study marine biodiversity and conservation opens up new avenues for research and understanding. Rather than viewing marine environments as simple input-output systems, adopting a quantum perspective allows for recognizing complex adaptive systems with emergent quantum-like macroscopic properties. This shift in perspective provides exciting opportunities for research and conservation efforts compared to traditional frameworks.

Quantum-inspired research initiatives in UAE

The United Arab Emirates (UAE) is a leader in using methods inspired by quantum physics to research and protect sea life. With university connections and study money, the UAE is starting cross-field projects. These combine quantum things with biology to find new skills in ocean life systems.

For example, scientists at NYU Abu Dhabi are looking into possible quantum stuff in the thinking and learning of sea mammals. They're also studying how they migrate or change according to weather conditions. These scientists want to learn more about marine animals' reactions and actions in response to environmental changes using ideas from quantum physics.

At Khalifa University, experts are creating new quantum-inspired ideas to study how coral reef communities work. Coral reefs are susceptible to turning white because of weather changes. It's essential to know how strong they can be so we can protect them better. Scientists want to use ideas inspired by quantum physics. They hope this will help them understand coral reef systems better and make plans to keep them safe.

As marine conservation gets more crucial, using tools and ideas that include quantum is becoming very necessary. As people keep putting enormous pressure on ocean life with things like climate change, pollution and breaking down habitats for fishing or other reasons - we need new ways to help these creatures in the sea.

Quantum technology can help us watch and understand marine life better. Sophisticated sensors and models based on quantum ideas can give more precise details. This allows scientists to make intelligent choices about saving nature. Using quantum tools, scientists can learn more about the complicated relationships inside ocean ecosystems. This helps improve efforts to protect them better.

So, using ideas similar to quantum physics in studying and protecting marine life is an ample opportunity. When we learn how fish swim using quantum methods and look the same in tiny plant-like ocean creatures, these new techniques teach us more about life underwater. The UAE's commitment to quantum and biology is shown through its efforts to bring together different fields. These actions aim to teach ways of keeping things safe in the area and worldwide. As we deal with environmental problems, tools and ways of thinking from quantum physics will be very important in keeping delicate sea creatures safe. This includes making sure that the oceans last a long time as well.

The UAE's Promise to Learn About and Protect Ocean Ecosystems

The United Arab Emirates (UAE) has become a big name worldwide for supporting eco-friendly growth and protecting ocean life. The UAE is working hard to save sea life. They do research, make new technology and help businesses work together with the government's goals in mind. In this way, they also balance making money while protecting nature well enough for future generations!

International Scientific Research Collaborations

Understanding that learning more about ocean environments is essential, the UAE works with other countries to study oceans together. A good team-up is between the Mohamed bin Zayed University of Artificial Intelligence (MBZUAI) and Saudi Arabia's KAUST research university. Together, they are looking at using intelligent computer programs to study sea life. This includes using computers to find out what kind of animal it is and check on the health of its population. Using AI technology, scientists can collect valuable information to help protect marine life and ensure ocean ecosystems last for a long time.

Groundbreaking Oceanography Expeditions

The UAE has made a big difference in helping to pay for essential ocean studies. For example, the Australasian Antarctic Expedition plans to look at and record particular life forms found in Earth's Southern Oceans. The UAE helps us learn about far-away ocean areas by backing these trips. It also assists in finding ways to keep these delicate ecosystems safe.

Domestic Initiatives for Marine Conservation

In the UAE, it is greatly supported to save marine life in different ways. The UAE Dolphin Project by the Emirates Natural History Group is a big job. It studies dolphins and whales in local waters. If scientists observe these types of animals, they can get essential details to help make laws and save them. These efforts show the UAE's dedication to preserving its own sea life and helping with world efforts to protect oceans.

Corporate Initiatives for Ecosystem Restoration

The UAE has not only done research and made policies but has also taken action in business to help bring back damaged ocean environments. Fujairah Adventures, a company from the UAE, started the Dibba Pearl Oyster Reef Project. This plan focuses on fighting the impacts of coral lightening by making fake reefs that help restore real ones. By making a home for sea creatures, these artificial reefs fix broken natural systems and help make the underwater world more robust and healthier.

Bold Policy Actions for Marine Protection

The UAE has shown it's ready to fight ocean damage. They have made solid rules for their own country and worldwide, too. The UAE knew that single-use plastics were terrible, so they stopped using them. This helped to cut down on trash ending up in the sea. The UAE strongly opposes harmful fishing methods such as shark finning. They promote sound environmental practices and support the protection of sea creatures in danger. The country has also led world plans, like the United Nations Ocean Science Decade. They are pushing for people to work together across countries and help save our ocean better.

Harnessing Quantum Technologies for Marine Biology

The UAE doesn't just use current tech; it also accepts breakthroughs to make it more robust as a leader in sustainability. The USA's plan to study oceans using quantum science shows its dedication. It looks at how these advanced technologies can be used to study sea life and protect it from danger. By using the power of quantum computing and other things called "quantum technologies", scientists can solve challenging problems about protecting our ocean resources. So, by working with other researchers and going on new trips at home for big companies or governmet action while also looking into tiny things called quantum technologies, the UAE has proven itself to be a world-famous leader in trying to protect our ocean's health. The UAE shows a good mix of growing its economy while looking after nature. This gives other people ideas to do the same in an environmentally-friendly way. By doing these things, the UAE keeps its sea creatures safe. It also helps save animals worldwide and ensures our oceans are healthy for a long time to come.

Challenges in Quantum Exploration of the Oceans

Advancing the futuristic vision of quantum exploration of the oceans has necessarily required overcoming several challenges along the way. The world's oceans impose disturbing and unforgiving situations on emerging quantum technology. In this article, we will discover a number of the important challenges confronted in the quantum exploration of the oceans and the way researchers and policymakers have worked to triumph over them.

Challenges in Quantum Gravimeters at Sea

One of the most demanding situations confronted in the quantum exploration of the oceans is the accuracy barriers of early quantum gravimeters because of vibrations and motions at sea. Unlike on land, where vibrations are much less typical, the sea environment poses particular challenges for quantum gravimeters. To overcome this, researchers have advanced adaptive isolation structures and pioneered solid-country quantum sensor designs that provide advanced vibration resistance. These improvements have extensively improved the accuracy and reliability of quantum gravimeters at sea.

Underwater Navigation with Quantum Gyroscopes

Another challenging issue of quantum exploration within the oceans is underwater navigation. Unlike on land, wherein GPS structures can provide particular place information, the dearth of GPS underwater makes navigation especially tough. To address this undertaking, essential improvements like quantum-enabled inertial steering systems have been developed. These systems make use of quantum gyroscopes to provide accurate navigation statistics, allowing researchers to discover the depths of the ocean with greater precision.

Translating Quantum-Theoretical Models into Conservation Insights

Researchers in search of adopting quantum-stimulated perspectives in marine conservation face the undertaking of translating complex quantum-theoretical fashions into tangible insights and rules. This calls for collaboration among multidisciplinary teams comprising marine biologists, ecologists, computer scientists, biophysicists, and quantum theorists. These groups work collectively to bridge the distance between abstract ideas and on-the-floor practice, permitting the improvement of conservation techniques based on quantum-better insights.

Updating Regulations for Responsible Quantum-Powered Marine Science

As quantum-powered advances in marine science continue to spread, policymakers face the undertaking of updating regulations to house those new abilities. The responsible use of strong quantum sensing, surveillance, and imaging abilities calls for the implementation of up-to-date ethical requirements. Policymakers have worked diligently to make certain that these advancements are used responsibly, protecting marine ecosystems as well as harnessing the capacity of quantum technologies to strengthen clinical information.

The UAE's Leadership in Overcoming Challenges

Fortunately, the UAE has shown agile governance and a way of life of embracing trade and continuous development, effectively adapting to the demanding situations posed by the quantum exploration of the oceans. The USA has implemented marine conservation rules based on novel quantum-improved insights into the fame of fragile ecosystems, together with coral reefs. Additionally, up-to-date ethics requirements have been installed to ensure responsible use of quantum technologies in marine technological know-how.

Future challenges and collaborative opportunities

While giant progress has been made, ongoing challenges remain in the quantum exploration of the oceans. Expanding quantum computing strength for advanced marine biology simulations is an essential place of cognizance. Additionally, fostering deeper collaboration among academia and enterprise is essential to translating essential quantum studies into extensive actual-international effect. The UAE's decisive management in technology, era, and sustainability positions the United States at the leading edge of overcoming those hurdles on a worldwide level.

Therefore, the quantum exploration of the oceans offers unique, demanding situations that require modern answers. From improving the accuracy of quantum gravimeters at sea to growing underwater navigation systems and translating complex quantum-theoretical models into conservation insights, researchers and policymakers have made great developments. The UAE's dedication to embracing trade and non-stop improvement has established the UAE as a leader in overcoming those challenges and leveraging the capability of quantum technology in marine science. As advancements hold, collaboration among academia, industry, and policymakers can be crucial to unlocking the total ability of quantum exploration within the oceans.

Vision 2050: Quantum-Inspired Sustainable Oceans

Looking towards the year 2050, the UAE's Quantum Exploration of the Oceans agenda sets a transformative Vision for marine sustainability. By seamlessly integrating quantum science into oceanographic research, conservation initiatives, resource management, and governance, a future of healthy, understood, and valued oceans comes into reach.

Cutting-edge quantum sensing, quantum machine learning, and quantum simulations will provide unmatched insights into marine ecosystems at all scales, biodiversity patterns, climate linkages, and natural resource mapping. For example, researchers envision expansive real-time quantum sensor networks autonomously monitoring ocean dynamics and pollution in high resolution across entire regions. Meanwhile, through detailed simulations, powerful quantum computers will enable an understanding of intricately complex marine food webs, fisheries populations, and cascading climate change impacts.

These quantum-powered advances will, in turn, drive more scientifically informed policymaking to manage critical ocean resources like fisheries in sustainable manners while protecting fragile ecosystems. Quantum-based tracking and monitoring technologies will also provide governments and corporations with vastly enhanced capabilities to respond to oil spills, track endangered marine species, detect toxic algal blooms, and survey the scale of plastic pollution across the oceans. On the economic front, the quantum era's profound knowledge of marine natural resources will promote next-generation green industries, renewable ocean energy, decarbonized marine transportation, and environmentally regenerative urban development along coastlines.

With pioneering nations like the UAE leading global cooperation, quantum science unlocks the promise of a sustainable blue economy in proper balance and harmony with ocean ecosystems. By 2050, quantum-inspired breakthroughs can reverse centuries of marine environmental degradation, restoring biodiverse and productive oceans valued both economically and ecologically.

Overall, the UAE's embrace of Quantum Exploration of the Oceans represents a visionary and pioneering step towards an enlightened, sustainable future. Responsibly leveraging quantum sensing, computing, AI, and quantum-inspired perspectives will profoundly expand humanity's scientific understanding of marine biology, ecology, natural resources, and vulnerabilities.

As a recognized global leader, the UAE is advancing quantum oceanography through research collaborations, conservation initiatives based on quantum monitoring, and evolving policies adapted to quantum capabilities. However, challenges inevitably remain in translating quantum innovations into tangible environmental and economic impact. The UAE's Vision 2050 provides an ambitious yet achievable quantum science and technology target to enable effective marine environmental stewardship. With ongoing progress in fundamental quantum research, commercialization efforts, updated policies, and multidisciplinary collaboration, the country is charting a course towards sustainably managed and valued ocean ecosystems.

The dawn of Quantum Exploration of the Oceans inaugurates an exciting era of transformative insights into marine biology and ecology for conservation and sustainable development. Combined with the UAE's ethos of knowledge-driven progress, the rise of quantum oceanography propels humanity towards a deeper relationship with our invaluable oceans in harmony with broader national and global ambitions for prosperity. The UAE is pioneering this quantum oceanography revolution.

CHAPTER 15

QUANTUM-INSPIRED URBAN PLANNING

We get on this enlightening journey and cast our lens on the mesmerizing cityscapes of the United Arab Emirates. However, the UAE is characterized by its relentless pursuit of innovation. It is harnessing the power of Quantum Management to craft a vision of smart, sustainable cities. Yet, redefine its urban lands. The dazzling dance between technology, innovation, and urban planning is the bedrock of this section.

Thus, Quantum-Inspired Urban Planning marries the principles of Quantum Mechanics with the exigencies of urban growth. This concept envisions urban spaces that intelligently adapt and respond to the requirements of inhabitants. They foster growth, sustainability, and a better life quality. This approach is about deploying insights from quantum science to craft cityscapes. They are aesthetically efficient and sustainable.

But the story does not end there; Quantum Management is integral to this process, a revolutionary approach that can potentially transform traditional urban planning models. This technique considers the inherent uncertainties and variables of city planning, allowing for more adaptable, dynamic, and future-ready urban spaces.

Let us delve deeper into Chapter 15 and explore this inspiring intersection of quantum theory and urban planning. We will also discover how the UAE's cities of the future are being shaped now. Reimagine skylines under the transformative influence of quantum. Shaping a future where cities are smarter, more livable, and sustainable truly.

Cityscapes Through Quantum-Inspired Architecture

Quantum principles have opened new doors and paved the way for innovative architectural design approaches in urban planning. The marriage of quantum theory and architecture results in cities that are more adaptable, efficient, and attuned to the changing needs of their inhabitants. Below are some key aspects in which quantum principles influence architectural design in urban planning:

1. **Probabilistic Design**: Quantum mechanics works on the principles of probabilities and uncertainties. In architecture, this can translate into designs considering all possible scenarios and outcomes, allowing flexibility and adaptability. It helps overcome unforeseen challenges and accommodate urban societies' evolving needs.

2. **Dynamic Connectivity**: Quantum phenomena such as entanglement inspire the creation of connected, interdependent spaces within urban environments. With entangled components, changes in one part of the system can ripple through and influence the remainder. The interconnection can lead to more cohesive and efficient presence.

3. **Superposition and Parallelism**: It allows particles to exist in multiple states simultaneously. While parallelism enables them to interact across various tracks. Incorporating these principles in architectural design can create multi-functional spaces and structures. It effectively caters to an urban population's diverse wishes.

4. **Tunneling Effect**: It is the phenomenon where particles pass through barriers that classical physics deems dreadful. However, this notion can inspire designs that break traditional boundaries and limitations in urban planning. It promotes innovative thinking and opening up new possibilities for spatial procedure.

5. **Quantum-inspired Materials**: Quantum science has led to the discovery of groundbreaking materials with advanced properties. Using these architectural materials can lead to buildings outperforming traditional structures in energy consumption.

6. **Adaptive Systems**: Quantum mechanics has inspired architects to develop adaptive systems that can learn from their surroundings. These systems can intelligently modify various building elements. It includes lighting, ventilation, and energy management to offer unparalleled comfort.

Innovations in Quantum-Inspired Architecture

As Quantum-Inspired Architecture is an emerging field. It blends cutting-edge quantum principles and innovative architecture, pushing the boundaries of traditional architectural design. Let's explore some key innovations:

Sustainability Advancements

These architectures champion the concept of sustainability, integrating environment-friendly solutions into their designs:

- **Renewable Energy Integration**: Quantum-inspired architecture encourages the use of renewable energy sources. For example, buildings harness solar power for electricity and wind energy for cooling systems.
- **Green Materials Usage**: Eco-friendly materials help minimize environmental impact. From using low-VOC paints and finishes to recycled materials, these architectures prioritize sustainability.
- **Green Spaces**: Incorporating vegetation into building designs, such as green roofs and wall gardens, supports biodiversity and enhances air quality within urban spaces.

Energy Efficiency Enhancements

Quantum concepts are ideally suited to improve energy efficiency:

- **Smart Energy Management**: Leveraging the idea of Quantum Tunneling, buildings can minimize energy loss through thermal insulation. Also, using adaptive systems, energy usage can be optimized based on factors like occupancy, time of day, or weather conditions.
- **Advanced Materials**: Buildings might use quantum-inspired materials like photovoltaic cells and thermochromic glass, promoting energy conservation.
- **Efficient Energy Storage**: Inspired by quantum mechanics, new energy storage methods, like Quantum Batteries, promise faster charging and higher energy densities, thus increasing energy efficiency.

Aesthetic Innovations

Quantum-inspired architecture challenges the norms of aesthetic design:

- **Fluid and Dynamic Designs**: Drawing from quantum superposition and wave-particle duality principles, architects now create buildings with dynamic, non-linear designs.
- **Light and Shadow Play**: Building design can manipulate light, creating fascinating light effects, shadows, and reflections, enhancing the visual appeal.
- **Interactive Facades**: Quantum principles inspire architects to design reactive facades that respond to various environmental conditions, changing their appearance based on sunlight, temperature, or wind direction.

Quantum-Inspired Iconic Buildings in UAE

No doubt, the UAE is known for its extravagant architecture. It is pushing the limits of design and novelty. Iconic buildings and urban spaces in UAE showcase futuristic and fluid designs that resonate with the principles of quantum mechanics. For example!

1. **Burj Khalifa, Dubai**: It is the tallest building in the world. It exhibits advanced structural engineering and innovative design techniques. Also, it defies traditional architectural boundaries

2. **Louvre Abu Dhabi**: The Louvre Abu Dhabi is designed by Jean Nouvel. It features a complex geometric dome. It allows for controlled light penetration. Also, echoing wave-particle duality and superposition principle.
3. **Aldar Headquarters**, **Abu Dhabi**: The first circular skyscraper in the Middle East has a unique geometry. It is breaking away from traditional box-shaped architecture.

Heightening Urban Efficiency and Sustainability

UAE city planners anticipate better and prepare for urban needs. It includes traffic flow and energy demand. They are contributing to heightened efficacy. Quantum principles promulgate a more interconnected circular approach. Here resources are utilized to their full potential. Thus, waste is reduced and environmental impact is diminished. Embracing such a fluid perspective Dubai and Abu Dhabi are continually pushing towards smarter and sustainable environments.

UAE's Strategies

UAE has implemented various strategies to enhance resource management, reduce waste, and promote green urban spaces.

In the construction industry, Dubai leads the path in promoting minimal resource usage and comprehensive waste recycling throughout all construction phases. The city's comprehensive green building strategy sets high sustainability standards and provides a remarkable example for cities worldwide.

The UAE has also launched a global initiative called "Waste to Zero." This endeavor aims to heighten the decarbonization efforts in waste management and the circular economy, striving towards the Paris Agreement's goal of reducing emissions by 43% by 2030.

Additionally, the UAE has a long-standing national campaign promoting a green economy and sustainable development by constructing green buildings and towns.

Finally, the Integrated Waste Management Strategy 2021-2041 encourages waste management, recycling, and energy conversion innovation. This approach involves implementing long-term projects to provide practical solutions for environmental challenges.

There are growing examples of cities incorporating quantum-inspired practices to boost efficiency:

Masdar City, Abu Dhabi: This city is built from scratch. It is a pioneer in sustainable urban progress. The design introduces quantum inspired principles to optimize resource usage. Its energy efficiency is optimized using smart building design and technology.

Dubai: Dubai Smart City employs quantum-inspired optimization algorithms for sustainable urban development. The city has implemented an advanced traffic system using these principles to control and predict traffic conditions, enhancing efficiency and reducing emissions. The concept is also applied to support waste management.

Sharjah: Sharjah uses quantum-inspired practices in its sustainable city project, particularly regarding optimizing resource use and waste management, furthering its sustainability initiatives.

Creating Cities That Resonate with the Pulse of Quantum Innovation

Quantum innovation can disrupt how we run our urban spaces, from traffic control to waste management and energy conservation. Here are a few examples of initiatives that incorporate quantum innovation:

The integration of smart technologies, IoT, and quantum-driven solutions.

Smart technologies: These technologies use digital technology, AI, and big data to meet people needs. It can optimize traffic flow and improve waste management. It also reduces energy consumption to make cities more sustainable.

Internet of Things (IoT): Thus, IoT is all about the interconnection of computing devices in everyday objects. It sends and receives data. The backbone of smart cities enabling efficient data collection and remote monitoring of systems. Energy grids to water provisions.

Quantum-driven solutions: Quantum computing can process vast amounts of data significantly faster than classical computers. It can be used to calculate the optimal routes for waste collection trucks or design models to predict energy consumption effectively.

Quantum Smart Infrastructure for Sustainable Cities

Quantum computing, with its exceptional ability to process complex variables in parallel, enhances the precision and efficiency of managing energy grids. Quantum algorithms can process vast amounts of data from diverse energy sources in real time, optimizing energy distribution and significantly reducing energy loss.

Certainly, let's delve into these three aspects:

Smart Grids: Transforming traditional energy infrastructure by incorporating:

- real-time data analytics
- automation
- renewable energy integration

Defined by the United States Department of Energy as an intelligent electricity grid, a smart grid uses digital communications technology and information systems. The automation detect and react to local changes in usage. It improves system operating efficiency and reducing operating expenses.

Efficient Transportation Systems: Technologies are being deployed in the context of smart cities. It creates sustainable transportation grids and revolutionize people's commute. Integrating smart grid technology in public transport can manage the rising demand for efficient transportation.

Environmentally Friendly Urban Utilities: These integrate various smart technologies to optimize resource management and reduce environmental impact. For instance, incorporating real-time data analytics in utilities like water and waste management can significantly contribute to building eco-conscious urban communities. The smart grid concept promotes a greener future by enabling a cleaner future of energy.

Ornamental City Resilience and Sustainability Through Quantum Solutions

Applying quantum solutions for enhancing city resilience and sustainability is in the initial phases. Some promising strategies leverage quantum computing power to provide next-level urban productivities. Here are some of them:

Adaptive Urban Planning: Cities can intelligently plan and model their urban spaces by using quantum algorithms. It involves variables often too complex for classical computers to handle optimally. For example:

- Demographic shifts
- Economic trends
- Traffic patterns
- Environmental impacts

If efficiently done, this leads to more resilient urban structures. They can better cope with social and ecological variations.

Enhanced Public Utilities: Here, quantum technologies provide tools. It handles the complex optimization problems involved in public utilities supervision. Maximize the efficiency of waste and water management too. Also, energy grids and other public services. Thus, reducing the cities' environmental impact.

Optimized Transport Systems: Hence, traffic congestion and inefficient transportation contribute to greenhouse gas releases. With quantum-powered solutions, cities can predict and manage traffic patterns. They can optimize routes and reduce travel time. Thus, reducing carbon releases.

Intelligent Infrastructure Maintenance: However, quantum computing can model and predict potential infrastructure failures before they occur. It enables predictive maintenance and avoid service pauses. Significantly enhances the longevity of urban infrastructures! It limits resource expenditures associated with unexpected failures.

Climate Modelling: Quantum computers can run complex simulations more effectively than classical ones. These simulations can inform policymakers about the best courses of action when applied to climate data. Yet, it mitigates the impacts of climate change, for more sustainable and better equipped to handle climate strains.

Improved Security Systems: Robust cybersecurity measures in the interconnected smart cities of the future will be critical. QKD can vastly improve security levels. It protects cities against cyber threats and ensures the stable operation of critical digital substructures.

UAE's Vision for Smart Cities Powered by Quantum Innovations

The UAE plans to increase renewable energy and enhance efficiency areas where quantum algorithms can aid in optimizing smart grid acts. Important digitalization and enhanced cybersecurity are also envisioned. Quantum key distribution potentially plays a key part. However, Flagship programs such as the Quantum Computing Program at the Technology Innovation Institute (TII) have been established to foster research in quantum computing. It showcases the UAE's commitment to integrating quantum technology into future city set-up.

Government initiatives, policies, and investments in shaping smart urban landscapes

Smart Dubai Initiative: The Smart Dubai Initiative aims to transform Dubai into the world's smartest and happiest city by 2021. It was launched in 2013 by His Highness Sheikh Mohammed bin Rashid Al Maktoum. It is based on six dimensions:

- Smart economy
- Smart living
- Smart governance
- Smart environment
- Smart people
- Smart mobility

However, it focuses on driving the adoption and integration of smart technologies across various sectors. It includes transportation and infrastructure. Moreover, public safety and energy management too.

Abu Dhabi's 'Ghadan 21' program: Ghadan 21 is a three-year, AED 50 billion (USD 13.6 billion) investment program. It was launched in 2018 to drive Abu Dhabi's economic growth and progress. It emphasizes innovation, knowledge and research. Hub71, a technology ecosystem attracted global startups and tech companies to Abu Dhabi as a part of this program.

UAE Energy Strategy 2050: The plan aims to increase the country's reliance on clean energy sources and reduce its carbon track. It includes increasing the share of clean energy in the total energy mix to 50%. Also, improving energy efficiency by 40 percent. Smart grid practices and focus on renewable sources is significant in transforming the UAE's urban land.

UAE Artificial Intelligence Strategy: It incorporates AI across various sectors to enhance efficiency and improve the decision-making processes in industries.

Technology Innovation Institute (TII): TII aims to become a leading global research center in advanced expertise. It comprises seven research departments. Among, one is dedicated to Quantum Computing. Thus, TII builds a foundation for the UAE's smart urban landscape by fostering a research ecosystem.

The Future of Urban Living

The vision for UAE Quantum Cities aligns with its broader goal of becoming a global leader in innovation and smart city. Varying levels of emphasis are placed on quantum technology across specific city projects. The nation's commitment to harnessing the power of quantum computing is vibrant.

This is an in-depth exploration of the UAE's vision:

1. Integrating Quantum Computing into Smart City Infrastructure:
The UAE is looking to integrate quantum computing into its smart city infrastructure projects. Intelligent urban planning and resource management can benefit from quantum algorithms to optimize these actions.

2. Investing in Quantum Research and Development:
The UAE is encouraging research in quantum computing and quantum technologies by establishing TII and its Quantum Computing Program. It encourages collaboration between academia, industry, and government. It fosters an ecosystem that drives innovation and achieve the nation's vision.

3. Collaborating with Global Quantum Experts and Institutions:
Global quantum experts and institutions develop cutting-edge quantum technologies. It includes joint initiatives and partnerships with international conferences on quantum computing. It boosts local development and research. The landmark agreement between Abu Dhabi's Cryptography Research Centre and Yale University! It advances post-quantum cryptography study.

4. Implementing Quantum Technologies for National Security and Cybersecurity:
No doubt, the UAE is highly interested in utilizing quantum technology. It safeguard its digital infrastructure and sensitive data. QKD can be employed to significantly enhance the security of communication networks and encrypt sensitive information.

5. Developing Quantum Technologies for Industry Applications:
The nation aims to revolutionize these industries by relying on the advancements in quantum computing. It makes them more efficient, sustainable, and supple.

The long-term goals
The long-term goals of Quantum-Inspired Urban Planning represent a prodigious leap towards futuristic, sustainable, and technologically advanced cities. Quantum computing's extremely high computational power holds the potential to revolutionize urban design efficiency, optimizing resource allocation and infrastructure development. It allows city utilities and services to perform at peak while minimizing waste. A quantum-based approach in urban planning also paves the way for advanced sustainable practices, from optimizing renewable energy use to reducing waste, thus creating environment-friendly cities. Transportation and mobility, too, can be dramatically improved with quantum strategies that ease traffic management and reduce congestion. Quantum-inspired city infrastructure management can introduce smart lighting systems, advanced surveillance, and IoT integrations in public spaces. This innovative roadmap for urban settings can power economic growth by catalyzing technological advancement and attracting investments. Furthermore, the adoption of quantum technologies can create unprecedented cybersecurity in smart cities. Thus, Quantum-Inspired Urban Planning ushers in a vision of cities where technology and sustainability coexist in perfect efficiency, marking a stark transition into a future built on quantum brilliance.

Overall , the transformative impact of Quantum-Inspired Urban Planning is key, underscoring a paradigm shift towards building more sustainable, efficient, and smart cities. This shift dramatically alters the traditional concepts of urban living, urging us to imagine cities where technology and sustainability aren't just woven into the fabric of urban life but are fundamental to its design and operation.

As we move forward from urban planning to the other aspects of Quantum Management in the subsequent chapters, we will continue to explore the UAE's ambitious journey. Driven by the vision of becoming a global leader in the quantum tech space, collectively, we'll unearth how these developments are set to catapult the UAE into a future where quantum technology is integral to its national identity and progress. This profound exploration throws light on the groundbreaking changes Quantum Management is on course to bring in multiple sectors as the UAE aligns itself with the dawn of the quantum era.

CHAPTER 16

QUANTUM GAMING AND ENTERTAINMENT REVOLUTION

D o you know that the emerging quantum era is at the cusp of revolutionizing the gaming and entertainment industries? Stepping into the destiny, the United Arab Emirates (UAE), with its function as a main international hub for technological innovation, is in a perfect place to ride this quantum wave and champion new-age immersive stories. The UAE government has clearly emphasized developing capabilities in quantum information science as a key pillar of its National Innovation Strategy. By making calculated investments on quantum R&D, recruiting top global talent, and forming partnerships with leading entertainment technology companies, the country will become a hub for innovative quantum-enabled media experiences.

This chapter is a look at how quantum technologies will play roles in transforming the gaming and entertainment industries. It presents how quantum technologies will influence gaming encounters, developments in immersive experiences and virtual worlds, and the UAE's endeavors to develop itself as a hub for entertainment driven by quantum power. Along with this, there is also discussion about obstacles that were encountered while developing new ideas for powered games using quantum.

The Quantum Leap in Gaming:

Quantum computing represents a revolutionary departure from classical binary computing by leveraging quantum mechanical phenomena like superposition and entanglement. Qubits exist in a superposition of 0 and 1, enabling exponential expansion in information density compared to binary bits. When clustered into quantum processors, qubits can perform highly parallelized computations ideal for complex simulations, optimization, and machine learning. While universal error-corrected quantum computers may be years away, significant advances have already been made in building specialized quantum processors offering a definitive speed-up over classical systems for niche applications. Global tech giants like IBM, Google, Microsoft, and startups like D-Wave and Rigetti have all built early quantum computers with 10-100 qubits.

Furthermore, The gaming industry is eagerly exploring routes to harness quantum computing for next-gen experiences. Key areas of promise include:

Photorealistic Graphics:

Quantum processor units designed for parallel graphics processing can render cinematic-quality visuals by crunching millions of polygons, textures, and shaders in real-time. Reduced pop-in, smooth dynamic lighting, and shadows powered by quantum computing will make game visuals more immersive.

Complex Physics:

Quantum simulations can accurately model particle interactions and fluid/smoke mechanics to boost game physics fidelity. Developers can build destructible, dynamically responsive worlds obeying quantum rather than approximated principles.

Sophisticated Game AI:

Quantum machine learning algorithms like Q-learning can rapidly process gameplay data to train reactive NPCs that adapt to player strategies. Quantum neural networks will also excel at forecasting to simulate realistic character decision trees during gameplay.

Limitless World Generation:

Combining quantum random number generation with quantum optimization can massively accelerate the procedural generation of expansive, detailed game worlds with unique textures, terrains, and functioning ecosystems.

Branching Interactive Narratives:

Quantum computing enables exponentially more narrative possibilities than classical binary choices. This results in stories adaptable to player agency with meaningful branching reflective of playstyle.

However, multiple engineering challenges remain, including quantum noise, error rates, and the extreme cooling required. Ongoing hardware and software R&D aims to address these obstacles through innovations like quantum error correction. Cloud access to quantum processors also lowers the barriers for gaming companies to experiment.

For developers, quantum computing allows reimagining fundamental gameplay mechanics, AI behaviors, and interactive narratives but requires investments in specialized quantum programming skills. For players, the quantum advantage unlocks more immersive visuals, smarter NPC interactions, and dynamic branching storylines tailored uniquely to every playthrough.

Quantum computing promises a transformative leap for gaming; just as 2D sprites transitioned to 3D polygons, the quantum era could lift creative possibilities beyond binary limits. As quantum processors mature over the next decade, gaming will likely emerge as one of the first domains ready to practically harness quantum's exponential speed-up to chart the future of interactive entertainment.

Transforming the Gaming and Entertainment Industry with Quantum Technologies

Quantum computing and related developments in quantum technology will have a lasting impact on the gaming sector as well. Quantum processors will transform the industry within three critical dimensions thanks to exponential growth in computational power and advanced algorithms dedicated to utilizing the quantum advantage.

Hyper Realistic Simulations:

Quantum processors' exceptional computational capabilities will make gaming and entertainment more realistic than ever before. The advantages of quantum algorithms allow developers to develop the most detailed physics models with predictive AI systems and complex world simulations. Think about a game where every object behaves under physics laws as if it were in the real world. Quantum computing will take hyperrealism to this level, allowing gamers a fully immersive experience where the difference between virtual and real life is blurred.

For instance, consider a car racing game scenario where the behavior of each car is not only dictated by predefined values but also through real-time computations that factor in wind resistance, grip on their tires, and so forth. With this quantum computing, the physics interactions can be effectively simulated in an accurate manner to form a truly lifelike driving game.

Immersive Environments:

Quantum sensing, imaging, and visualization technologies will be the key enablers for next-generation immersive platforms like augmented reality AR VR or mixed reality MR. These technologies will allow developers to develop a full spectrum of experiences that also interact with all human senses and take users into completely different worlds.

For example, quantum imaging in AR applications allows easy integration of virtual objects with the real world, giving users a more realistic and immersive experience. In addition, quantum computing can improve VR games by creating high-resolution and dynamic virtual spaces in which players interact with objects or characters that respond realistically using the principles of quantum algorithms.

Adaptive Gameplay:

Quantum machine learning and quantum AI models will give developers the power to develop games or experiences that change based on player choices, styles of play, emotions, and also situational context. Quantum computing can help games adapt their narratives, gameplay mechanics, and difficulty levels in an almost real-time manner so that each player gets personalized feedback.

Suppose a role-playing game in which the plot unfolds itself differently depending on the decisions made by the player. Quantum machine learning makes it possible for the game to analyze a player's choices, emotions, and playing style and create an individual story line based on their preferences. This degree of adaptability will engage players, making each gaming session truly personal.

Leading companies such as Ubisoft have already established labs dedicated to the research of quantum techniques that could be used for establishing greater realism in their games' simulation. Even tech giants like Microsoft, Google, and IBM, as well as startups such as QCWare, are actively finding the use of quantum-enhanced design workflows in gaming applications.

As quantum computing platforms continue to develop over the next ten years, they will open doors in areas of realism, dynamism, and immersion that once seemed impossible if classical techniques were relied upon. This will forever revolutionize the gaming and entertainment industry, providing users with experiences that make it difficult to differentiate virtual from reality. Quantum is the future of gaming, and it has unlimited potential.

Quantum Computing Empowered Immersive Experiences and Virtual Realms

Quantum computing is soon going to reinvent the world of immersive experiences and virtual realms, providing never-before-seen levels of authenticity and interactivity. Developers will be able to create virtual reality that engages all human senses and provides true immersion using quantum technologies.

One of the main areas where quantum computing can be applied to immersive experiences is in generating photorealistic 3D environments. Quantum simulation techniques enable the rendering of detailed and intricate virtual worlds on the fly. The level of detail and realism that can be achieved when using traditional rendering methods is very time-consuming from the computational side. Nevertheless, utilising quantum computing allows developers to model how light behaves along with materials at a quantum level, and this process can create incredibly realistic graphics.

Quantum Machine Learning for Reactive NPCs

Quantum machine learning models are helpful in populating virtual worlds with non-player characters (NPCs) that can have intricate behaviors and interact with the environment and players realistically and dynamically. These NPCs may converse meaningfully, react to the player's actions, and modify their behavior depending on what happens in this virtual world. Quantum algorithms can allow for the training of machine learning models more quickly and efficiently, which in turn allows for NPCs that are quicker to respond as well as smarter.

Quantum entanglement networks can transform collaborative experiences in virtual domains. Developers are able to create distributed metaverse environments where users from different locations can interact and collaborate in real-time by taking advantage of the principles associated with quantum entanglement. This marks the beginning of a new era for social interaction, multiplayer gaming, and virtual events that enable an effortless feel and an immersive experience for their participants.

Quantum Computing Partnerships

Leading quantum algorithm firms, like QC Ware, are actively researching the uses of quantum computing in creating digital humans and special metaverse experiences. These partnerships between consumer virtual reality and augmented reality platforms, such as Meta Quest, are laying the groundwork for incorporating quantum technologies into general entertainment. By coupling the capabilities of quantum computing to consumer-grade VR AR technology, developers can produce astonishing and indelible virtual experiences.

Quantum computing can also considerably increase the capabilities of reinforcement learning algorithms, allowing for better game AI and more complex response patterns. Reinforcement learning algorithms have been shown to be up to 100 times faster in training time by porting them onto current quantum processors, according to Google AI researchers. This feature enables game developers to develop smarter and more adaptive virtual opponents, thereby improving the enjoyment of the gaming experience.

Also, the combinatorial explosion enabled by quantum computers allows the scope of world simulation and procedural content generation to be significantly increased. Essentially, this opens up the possibility for developers to make adjustable virtual worlds and RPGs with virtually limitless potential for replay value. Each play-via may be special, permitting gamers to get a fully realistic and customized gaming experience.

Overall, quantum computing promises to revolutionize the gaming and enjoyment enterprise with more advantageous immersion, realism, and interactivity. Quantum technologies promise a brand new frontier for developers within the advent of charming and unforgettable digital geographical regions by means of bringing together photorealistic environments, reactive NPCs, collaborative metaverse reports, more desirable procedural content material era, and many others. For example, within the close to future, we can witness an exciting merger of quantum and enjoyment technologies with a purpose to alternate how video games and digital reports are processed.

Positioning the UAE as a Hub for Quantum-Powered Entertainment

The UAE is aggressively positioning itself at the forefront of quantum innovation through investments in research, infrastructure, and human capital development.

The Mohamed Bin Zayed University of Artificial Intelligence has partnered with tech leaders like Google to develop quantum computing skills locally. Dubai's World Trade Centre hosts QCC, the region's first quantum computing commercialization center. Abu Dhabi's Advanced Technology Research Council (ATRC) is also funding quantum startup incubators and university research grants. By proactively fostering a thriving ecosystem for quantum R&D and instituting policies that attract global entertainment studios, the nation can establish itself as the leading hub for quantum gaming and immersive media in the Middle East.

Global partnerships via organizations like BRIDGING will also drive the UAE's quantum entertainment agenda. Initiatives like QCC's virtual gaming metaverse built on Quantum Origin's platform highlight early steps being taken. To lead the quantum entertainment revolution, the UAE must link its entertainment, tech, and education sectors—fostering R&D, incubating startups, training specialized talent, and evolving the requisite infrastructure.

Challenges and Innovations in Quantum Gaming and Entertainment

While the long-term potential is compelling, engineering challenges remain to be addressed before quantum technologies permeate gaming and entertainment. Realizing the full potential of quantum computing for gaming faces critical challenges that ongoing research aims to overcome.

One major obstacle is that current experimental quantum processors are inherently noisy, leading to errors in calculated outputs. This noise arises from instability in maintaining the fragile quantum states of qubits. Various strategies are being explored to detect and account for errors, including quantum error correction codes that work by redundantly encoding information across multiple qubits. Error mitigation software techniques also show promise for obtaining usable outputs despite noise by exploiting algorithmic redundancies.

Another key challenge is seamlessly integrating quantum and classical computing components into hybrid systems. Since not all gaming computing tasks will require quantum power, optimally leveraging both quantum and classical hardware requires standardised frameworks for passing data that currently do not exist. Researchers are working on streamlining these interfaces between quantum and classical resources.

In addition, the extreme cryogenic cooling required to keep quantum processors in their stable operating states poses practical deployment hurdles. Reducing this cooling overhead is important for broad adoption outside laboratories. Hardware solutions being examined include novel qubit materials like diamond that exhibit greater temperature resilience.

On the innovation front, companies are pioneering qubit technologies involving exotic quantum materials that intrinsically have longer coherence lifetimes and lower error rates. Modular quantum processor architectures optimized for specific applications like optimization or simulation are also being designed. This can boost performance on gaming-centric workloads.

For software advances, error mitigation techniques are being implemented to obtain usable outputs despite noise by redundancy checking for errors. Hybrid quantum-classical algorithms that strategically minimize overall qubit usage to limit noise exposure also show promise. Libraries for quantum machine learning, vital for gaming AI, are areas of active refinement.

In summary, delivering the quantum advantage to transform gaming will require joint progress on hardware design, materials science, and algorithmic techniques. Gaming applications stand poised to reap the benefits as quantum technology matures over the next decade.

Vision 2050: Quantum-Enabled Entertainment Landscape

The UAE's Vision 2050 lays out the blueprint for a diversified, sustainable economy, with technology, education, and human capital development as its cornerstones. Quantum gaming and immersive media will be integral pillars of this vision's realization. By embracing quantum's disruptive potential early, the UAE can chart the trajectory of entertainment's evolution over the next quarter century.

Investment in infrastructure, R&D, and specialized talent today will position the nation as the de facto global hub for pioneering quantum media experiences by 2050. The seamless blending of physical and virtual worlds will become commonplace. Subscription-based services will provide access to limitless bespoke realities and simulation theory-grade immersion.

The economic impact will be manifold, with diverse job opportunities spanning quantum software development, interactive narrative design, and metaverse infrastructure. Augmented human co-experience and collaboration at a global scale. Ultimately, delivering profound insight into the human condition.

As concluded ,Quantum science promises to revolutionize gaming and entertainment by enabling unprecedented scales of simulated reality and immersion. Through proactive policies, investment in infrastructure and talent, and global collaboration, the UAE is poised to spearhead this entertainment transformation in the coming decades.

Human creativity will thrive by synergizing with computational capabilities inconceivable before the advent of quantum computing. The UAE's strategic embrace of quantum's disruptive innovation will pioneer the next major evolution in how humanity experiences virtual worlds, engages imagination, and pushes the frontiers of consciousness. This foundation sets the stage to further explore the nation's multidimensional quantum management framework across scientific, economic, industrial, and societal landscapes, ultimately propelling the UAE's vision to lead globally in the information age.

CHAPTER **17**

QUANTUM-INSPIRED PHILANTHROPY

Philanthropy has been a crucial device for fighting some of the most tremendous problems affecting humanity, together with getting rid of disease and assuaging poverty. On the other hand, an exceptional scale of technological growth in the twenty-first century now offers philanthropic initiatives a brand new opportunity to harness emerging innovations closer to deeper effect. One of such opportunities for completely rethinking philanthropic endeavors through what can be referred to as quantum-inspired philanthropy is the growth or ascendancy of quantum technologies.

Quantum-Inspired Philanthropy is the use of quantum principles, such as superposition, entanglement, and parallelism, to enable step-change advancements on a global scale in solving humanitarian issues. Advanced quantum technologies in computing, sensing, imaging, and communication can help optimize humanitarian operations to distribute resources efficiently so that delivery of healthcare innovations becomes possible, making data-driven philanthropic decisions more empowered.

As a major forerunner in quantum research, the United Arab Emirates is uniquely positioned to lead quantum-inspired philanthropy, merging its generous and philanthropic culture with national ambitions of leveraging technology-dedicated ness to achieve transformative social impact. The realization of this huge capacity calls for quantum technologies being incorporated into philanthropic initiatives, the establishment and alignment of global partnerships, and the capability to use quantum tools actively in order to raise levels of human welfare globally. Let's explore more through this chapter.

Leveraging Quantum Technologies for Impactful Philanthropic Endeavours:
Quantum technologies can dramatically enhance the effectiveness of philanthropic efforts across three key dimensions:

Optimized Humanitarian Operations:
Quantum computing introduces new capabilities to rapidly solve complex logistics challenges related to humanitarian operations through optimized scheduling, mapping, and pattern detection. For example, when responding to a natural disaster, quantum algorithms can parse massive datasets and variables in real-time to optimize dynamic relief supply routing, ensuring life-saving resources reach affected communities the fastest.

Quantum processors can also rapidly generate and analyze geospatial maps of regions struck by natural disasters to find optimal locations for temporary aid camps and medical facilities. By running disaster scenario simulations, quantum computers can reveal bottlenecks and inefficiencies in humanitarian workflow.

Secure communication is vital when coordinating multi-agency efforts across remote areas. Quantum encryption via unhackable cryptographic keys enables various humanitarian groups to securely share sensitive data and synchronize responses without compromise.

Efficient Resource Planning
Predicting needs and dynamically allocating resources is key to effective humanitarian delivery. Quantum simulation techniques can model probabilistic scenarios to forecast humanitarian demands in various crisis situations. This enables data-driven planning of relief resources and personnel.

Real-time tracking of aid distribution is crucial for accountability. Quantum sensors like lidar can achieve precise geospatial monitoring of supplies en route to their intended recipients. By flagging diversion or leakage, optimal allocation can be maintained.

Quantum machine learning applied to survey datasets can also rapidly predict which communities are most vulnerable to disasters, disease, or conflict. This allows targeting preventative interventions precisely to where needs are emerging.

Data-Driven Decision Making

Transforming humanitarian data into actionable insights is key for strategic policy decisions. Quantum AI methods can rapidly analyze complex humanitarian datasets—from refugee movements to healthcare access—to reveal correlations, trends, and predictive patterns difficult to discern through conventional analytics.

These data-driven insights, powered by quantum machine learning algorithms applied to multidimensional data, allow philanthropic leaders to take precise, evidence-based actions, be it forecasting outbreaks before they occur or modeling population vulnerabilities to calibrate interventions accordingly. Global instances validating quantum potential for philanthropy abound, from IBM's partnership with UNICEF leveraging quantum optimisation for improved aid delivery to Los Alamos National Lab demonstrating refugee camp planning using quantum annealing.

In summary, purposefully channeling quantum advances promises to supercharge philanthropic efficacy—uplifting human welfare globally through values-based innovation.

Innovative Approaches to Addressing Global Challenges

The unique capabilities unlocked by quantum technologies allow philanthropic initiatives to take creative new approaches to addressing diverse global challenges.

Efficient Disaster Response:

Quantum simulation of weather patterns, seismic models, and flood propagation dynamics can precisely forecast the timing, location, and severity of natural disasters even before they strike. Quantum computing can then optimize real-time disaster response logistics as the situation unfolds. Quantum cryptography enables secure humanitarian data sharing across response agencies. This allows mobilizing precisely the right life-saving resources to where they are needed most when disasters strike.

Targeted Poverty Alleviation:

Quantum machine learning applied to multidimensional poverty survey datasets can precisely identify root factors driving poverty across communities and forecast vulnerability risks at individual levels. This allows philanthropic interventions to be tailored with sociocultural nuance to address the needs, values, and risks of individual communities.

Transformational Healthcare:

Quantum computational simulations can accelerate pharmaceutical discoveries and clinical trial optimisations to deliver new life-saving drugs faster, especially for neglected diseases. Quantum bio-medical imaging enables rapid, accurate, and low-cost diagnosis. Quantum communication ensures healthcare data privacy. Together, this can drive leapfrog advances in healthcare access across regions.

The XPRIZE Foundation, focused on incentivizing technological solutions that benefit humanity, has emphasized the need to proactively leverage quantum advances, aptly capturing the ethos of quantum-inspired philanthropy.

The UAE's Contribution to a Quantum-Inspired Era of Giving:

The UAE is strategically pioneering quantum-inspired philanthropy both domestically and globally through numerous initiatives across the public, private, and non-profit sectors.

Mohammed Bin Rashid Global Initiatives Foundation

This organization is collaborating with quantum computing leaders like IBM to explore harnessing quantum capabilities for optimized humanitarian efforts. Focus areas include improving education access, healthcare delivery, and disaster response across the Middle East and Africa through quantum-powered logistics, forecasting, and data analytics.

Dubai Cares

Dubai Cares is an innovative philanthropic organization partnering with global aid agencies to pilot and deploy quantum-enabled solutions that enhance the impact and accountability of educational programs. This includes testing quantum machine learning to forecast regions at high risk of dropping literacy rates and quantify the success of interventions. Quantum computing is also being leveraged to optimize supply chains for textbook and resource delivery.

Emirates Red Crescent

The UAE's humanitarian arm is probing potential quantum applications in forecasting refugee crises, tracking aid supplies in real-time via quantum sensors, and simulating optimization scenarios for early resource mobilization using quantum computers. Advanced data analytics using quantum machine learning can also help reveal specific aid interventions that best serve displaced populations.

Abu Dhabi Global Market

This hub is collaborating with local quantum startups like Qilimanjaro Quantum Tech to drive innovations in quantum algorithms and simulation techniques that could expand data-driven insights for philanthropic decision-making. New quantum computational methods can reveal trends and patterns in humanitarian datasets that better inform aid planning.

Private Sector

UAE's private sector giants like Etisalat are sponsoring university research and hackathons to drive quantum computing projects with positive humanitarian impact. Areas range from quantum encryption to secure refugee data to quantum AI for medical relief forecasts. Such initiatives provide platforms and funding to catalyze quantum philanthropy.

Global Partnerships

The UAE is also forging partnerships with global philanthropic foundations like the Bill & Melinda Gates Foundation to jointly fund and pioneer quantum computing initiatives that can address humanitarian challenges in critical areas like hunger, preventable disease, and financial inclusion.

In summary, the UAE is pioneering quantum-inspired philanthropy globally by synergizing its generous culture with its technological vision. Strategic initiatives across sectors to explore, fund, and deploy quantum capabilities for humanitarian gain affirm the nation's commitment to serving humanity through values-based innovation.

Quantum-Driven Humanitarian Initiatives

Across humanitarian domains, tailored applications of quantum technologies can significantly optimize operations:

Disaster Response:

Quantum optimization of supply logistics, asset tracking using quantum sensors, and quantum-secured data sharing between relief agencies can dramatically improve disaster response efficiency. Training emergency responders in quantum technology is also vital.

Refugee/Displaced People Support: Quantum simulation of migratory flows, real-time tracking of aid supplies via quantum sensors, and optimized refugee camp planning enabled by quantum processors can enhance displaced population support.

Healthcare Interventions:

Quantum bio-medical imaging enables rapid diagnostics. Quantum machine learning helps forecast disease outbreaks and medicinal needs. Quantum computing accelerates clinical trials and drug development, saving lives. Expanding access to quantum healthcare innovations globally is key.

In the private sector, philanthropic foundations and technology leaders are coming together to drive these applications, like Cognite and SINTEF exploring quantum computing for streamlining Norwegian aid programs. Real-world humanitarian deployments will rapidly expand as the quantum ecosystem matures.

Challenges in Implementing Quantum-Inspired Philanthropy

Even though the potential of quantum-inspired philanthropy is enormous, there are several significant challenges to putting into practice this futuristic idea. There are various challenges, ranging from technological adoption barriers to ethical considerations and so on.

Integrating Quantum Technologies

It is not an easy task to integrate emergent quantum technologies in the context of large-scale philanthropic operations. Practical adoption of these technologies implies a huge amount of obstacles that have to be resisted, such as technical intricacies, financial aspects, and the willingness to consider return on investment. Due to the inherently disruptive nature of quantum technology, there may be a need for gradual deployment in order to ensure an effortless transition and effective use of these powerful tools. Organizations can use the tangible benefits and successful case studies to showcase confidence in adopting quantum technology for philanthropic initiatives.

Multilateral Collaborations

Strategic priorities, resource sharing, and the avoidance of duplicative efforts should be brought into alignment. Diplomatic skills will be vital in creating these collaborative ecosystems, ensuring that all participants contribute towards a unified cause. Organizations capable of establishing solid partnerships can utilize collective expertise and resources to tackle difficult challenges more efficiently.

Agility and Continuous Learning

With global challenges changing rapidly, quantum-led innovations in the philanthropic space must also change to stay relevant and impactful. Agility and the ability to adapt quickly are very important. Organizations should develop a culture of continuous learning and innovation where they are constantly looking for new knowledge and insights.

Ethical Considerations

Quantum capabilities for philanthropy at scale bring about ethical concerns that should be proactively tackled. Key ethical risks include data privacy, algorithmic bias, and intellectual property when using quantum technology. It is important to develop strong frameworks and guidelines that will protect individuals' privacy, ensure fairness in algorithmic decision-making, and encourage responsible use of intellectual property. By proactively dealing with such ethical concerns, the organizations would be able to make use of quantum technology for charitable purposes while maintaining all-round ethics and ensuring secure rights and dignity for the individuals involved.

In spite of these odds, the revolutionary move in the UAE to harmonize quantum investments with humanitarian goals offers a pathway past such difficulties via value-oriented innovations. Placing the focus on creating positive change and enhancing human welfare, such as in what is done by the UAE nowadays, shows a model for other nations and organizations to follow. If the UAE stays true to their values and uses quantum technology as a means of achieving their philanthropic goals, it proves that challenges can be conquered in order to benefit society if one possesses determination, strategic skill, and is focused on good.

Therefore, there are challenges attached to the implementation of quantum-inspired philanthropy. However, overcoming the adoption hurdles, promoting multilateral collaborations, adapting to agility and continuous learning, and focusing on ethics can ensure that quantum technology becomes a practical tool for philanthropic purposes. The values-based innovation approach of the UAE serves as a role model and demonstrates how others can overcome these challenges by successfully harnessing the potential of quantum technology for improving life on earth.

Reflection on Quantum-Inspired Philanthropy

Quantum-inspired philanthropy has the potential to profoundly amplify the UAE's contributions to global wellbeing. Leveraging quantum technologies aligns with the nation's humanitarian ethos and technological ambitions. Strategic investments to deploy quantum capabilities for philanthropic gain today will ensure the UAE continues to lead in addressing global challenges well into the future. Taking an ethics-first approach and rigorously evaluating initiatives' true impact will be critical.

Ultimately, spearheading quantum-inspired philanthropy could inspire a paradigm shift in humanitarian practices worldwide, catalyzing a new era of generosity, collaboration, and scientific optimism in service of humanity.

Vision 2050: Quantum-Driven Humanitarian Leadership

The United Arab Emirates' Vision 2050 not only creates the platform for continued leadership to guide humanity across the globe but also presents a novel approach using technology as an instrument of excellence. The concept of quantum-inspired philanthropy comes forth as an essential pillar in this grand vision, which has the potential to radically transform how humanitarian activities are carried out.

By investing wisely in quantum research, developments, and ecosystems, the UAE is now ensuring that by 2050 it will be a leader in quantum humanitarianism. Such forward thinking will allow the nation to create new solutions, build strong allies, and initiate powerful paradigms for applying science in the service of humanity.

The UAE is one of the pioneering countries that demonstrate a keen attitude towards quantum-inspired philanthropy, mainly due to the perception that modern technologies, including quantum computing and algorithms with analogous principles, might be able to not only solve but also prevent major problems on our planet. The nation aims to establish a quantum ecosystem that not only supports cutting-edge research but also ensures the practical deployment of quantum solutions by leveraging the potential of quantum mechanics.

This is a visionary approach that draws from the UAE's already established position as an example of value-driven innovation. The people of the nation have always been known to be generous, and they love adopting modern technology meant to enhance society. By combining its philanthropic efforts with its technological competencies, the UAE aims to promote human welfare and dignity across the world.

The incorporation of quantum-inspired philanthropy into the humanitarian efforts of the UAE will lead to innovative outcomes in all fields. The nation sees the enrichment of healthcare, education, agriculture, climate change mitigation, and disaster response, among others, with the use of quantum technologies. The opportunities are unlimited, and the UAE is committed to finding every chance for a brighter future for all.

Moreover, the UAE's focus on building partnerships will be crucial to its successful quantum-driven humanitarian leadership. Appreciating the value of collaboration, therefore, the country aims to form a world-wide community of compatible organizations and researchers as well as philanthropists. By promoting a collaborative atmosphere, the UAE seeks to speed up efforts to make quantum solutions more implementable and widespread so that people around the world can take advantage of their benefits.

With the UAE leading the way in quantum-driven humanitarian leadership, it paints a society where technology plays a role as an enabler for good. 2050 announces the nation's bold precedent for other regions of the world concerning merging science with philanthropy and compassion. The UAE is taking the lead in pioneering quantum-inspired philanthropy to usher in a new generation of innovation, which will be driven by technology that provides upward mobility and empowerment for communities worldwide.

So, the UAE's Vision 2050 accelerates the nation towards a future in which quantum-powered humanitarian leadership is in high gear. Through value-based innovation involving strategic investments and partnerships, the UAE seeks to uplift human welfare and dignity globally through quantum technologies. If the nation takes on this vision, it lays a path to an era full of compassion and technological advancements where quantum power fosters constructive changes for its posterity.

Quantum-inspired philanthropy offers an amazing chance for the UAE to take huge steps in solving global issues as it harnesses the power of quantum advancements with a humanitarian approach. To fully realize the benefits of this venture, the UAE must develop collaborative ecosystems actively, evaluate them correctly to get an accurate picture of how impactful their initiatives are or can be, and create cross-sector partnerships, enabling them with expertise and resources from other sectors during the development and engagement stages, which is vital for catapulting ideas successfully into the implementation stage, as well as as quantum technologies continue evolving. The UAE's role as the worldwide pilot of Quantum Inspired Philanthropy would enable it to introduce a new age of generous philanthropic ardor, powered by technology.

From the optimization of resource allocation to planning effective supply chains, quantum-inspired solutions can simplify operations and increase aid programme reach and effectiveness. When the UAE adopts quantum-inspired philanthropy, it not only gains ground as a global power in regards to humanitarian affairs but also sets an example for other countries. By dedicating itself to ethics-based innovation and accepting the potential of quantum technologies, the UAE can stimulate a fresh surge in philanthropic causes that use modern science as their ally for mankind's benefit.

CHAPTER 18

QUANTUM-SECURED COMMUNICATION NETWORKS

Communication networks are the spine of our hyper-connected world, which allows information to flow freely and quickly, driving modern society. With the scaling up of these networks, either in terms of scope or complexity, their security has never been more critical. Quantum technologies are revolutionary solutions to protect networks against growing threats in the age of data transmission everywhere. Quantum-secured communication protocols can offer nearly unbreakable encryption when based on the principles of quantum physics to protect confidential information.

The United Arab Emirates (UAE) has become a trailblazer in understanding the essential role quantum sciences play in generating innovation and establishing new infrastructure. The UAE government will equip communication systems across critical industries and departmental operations with quantum-safe security through a forward national agenda. This commitment to quantum management establishes the nation as a leader in developing and implementing ultra-secure communication networks for the future. Let's explore more about quantum-secured communication networks in this chapter.

Quantum Communication Protocols for Ultra-Secure Data Transmission

Quantum communication has emerged as a groundbreaking discipline that makes use of the standards of quantum mechanics to achieve extremely secure information transmission. Unlike classical communique strategies, which might be vulnerable to eavesdropping and hacking, quantum communique protocols ensure the confidentiality and integrity of transmitted information.

One of the largest applications of quantum communication is quantum key distribution (QKD). QKD permits events to safely alternate encryption keys with the aid of leveraging the particular houses of quantum debris. The fundamental concept at the heart of QKD lies in the reality that any attempt to measure or intercept quantum debris will necessarily disturb its quantum states. This disturbance serves as an indicator of external observation, enabling the communicating parties to detect any potential tampering with the transmitted data.

In 2016, the Dubai Electricity and Water Authority (DEWA) collaborated with the University of Dubai to pioneer one of the world's first urban QKD networks. The primary objective of this implementation was to enhance the security of communication within smart grid infrastructure. By utilizing QKD, DEWA aimed to protect critical power and water networks from cyber threats. This real-world application showcases the enormous value that quantum-secured communication brings to safeguarding infrastructure supporting vital services.

On the other hand, quantum communications have become a cutting-edge industry that leverages the principles of quantum mechanics to obtain super-secure data transmission. Unlike traditional modes of communication that are prone to eavesdropping and hacking, quantum communication protocols ensure the integrity and security of communicated information.

QKD is one of the most important uses for quantum communication. QKD enables two parties to securely share encryption keys using the peculiar properties of quantum particles. The basic principle of QKD stems from the fact that any effort to measure or intercept quantum particles will inevitably affect their quantum states. This disturbance is a sign of outward checking, allowing virtual communicants to access any possible interference with delivered information.

In 2016, Dubai Electricity and Water Authority partnered with the University of Dubai to establish one of the first urban QKD networks in the world. One of the key goals of this implementation was to improve communication security in smart grid infrastructure. DEWA intended to protect its critical power and water networks using QKD from potential cyber threats. This practical scenario highlights the huge value that quantum-secured communication provides when protecting goods in such infrastructure, as key services do not wish to be put at risk. Apart from QKD, nowadays many other systems of interaction based on quantum technologies are being tested and developed worldwide for various security concerns. One such protocol is quantum secure direct communication (QSDC), whereby a secret message itself can be encoded in various states of quanta. This is a unique characteristic that allows the encrypted data to be created and transmitted simultaneously without having to pass through steps of key distribution. QSDC is highly promising for use cases where real-time, secure communication is crucial.

Quantum digital signatures are another protocol that seems to be gaining attention. Further attempts to develop and improve upon new quantum communication protocols continue in the hope of making them more universal and applicable for different security needs. Researchers and scientists all around the world never stop advancing quantum mechanics to create new solutions that can change how we send and protect sensitive information.

 As such, quantum communication protocols, including QKD, QSDC, and quantum digital signatures, provide unprecedented security for data transmission. Implementing urban QKD networks such as those used by DEWA and the University of Dubai shows practical use for quantum communication for protecting essential infrastructure. There is huge potential for quantum communication to change the field of data protection and encryption as researchers continue research into new protocols.

Safely Preserving Critical Data in the Era of Quantum Computing

While enabling ultra-safe communication, quantum physics simultaneously threatens the effectiveness of traditional encryption methods. Running algorithms such as Shor's algorithm, quantum computers have the ability to crack commonly used public-key encryption schemes, which are responsible for securing data transmission today. As nation-states and organizations continue to advance quantum computing research, they edge closer to compromising the classical security standards relied upon by governments and businesses worldwide.

Recognising this looming threat, national cybersecurity authorities in the UAE have already begun transitioning to quantum-safe cryptographic standards to protect sensitive data. In 2021, the National Electronic Security Authority mandated government entities to implement post-quantum cryptography approved by national standards. These clear actions are evidence of the proactive approach that the UAE takes when it comes to building infrastructure prepared for the paradigm shift brought by quantum technologies.

As a matter of fact, experts are already forecasting that in the coming decade, quantum computers will have sufficient computing power to break very popular cryptographic schemes such as RSA and ECC. Their basis for security relies on the challenges that factoring large prime numbers and solving discrete logarithm problems pose.

However, Shor's algorithm running on a sufficiently powerful quantum computer could efficiently solve these mathematical problems, rendering RSA and ECC insecure.

To prepare for this eventuality, the UAE government has established research partnerships with universities to actively test and adopt new quantum-resistant encryption methods. Leading proposals for post-quantum cryptography include lattice-based cryptography and hash-based cryptography. Lattice-based schemes involve problems like the Learning with Errors problem, which quantum computers cannot currently solve efficiently. Hash-based cryptography uses hash functions rather than public-private key pairs to secure communications.

Proactively upgrading systems to use post-quantum encryption ensures the continuity of secure critical operations even as quantum computing capabilities advance. Financial institutions and digital infrastructure providers must also integrate quantum-safe cryptography to protect sensitive customer data and intellectual property from future attacks. Mandating these upgrades before the advent of capable quantum computers prevents a scenario where trillions of dollars and classified government secrets become vulnerable overnight.

Beyond upgrading encryption protocols, organizations should also employ quantum-secured communications leveraging quantum key distribution (QKD). Unlike classical encryption, which relies on computational hardness, QKD uses quantum physics properties like the no-cloning theorem to enable information-theoretically secure key exchange between parties. This protects against even a quantum computer breaking the mathematical assumptions underlying classical cyphers.

Installing QKD links in critical infrastructure like government data centres will future-proof confidentiality against advancing quantum and classical cyber threats. China already activated a 2,000-kilometre quantum-secured Beijing-Shanghai communication backbone in 2022, illustrating governmental initiatives worldwide to harness quantum technology for security.

Awareness and education are also pivotal for developing a quantum-ready workforce. Cybersecurity experts must understand new post-quantum cryptography primitives and transition strategies to upgrade systems seamlessly. Universities will need to equip computer science and engineering graduates with knowledge of quantum information theory and practical skills for implementing quantum-safe solutions.

Building human capital and upgraded infrastructure will enable the UAE to continue its leadership in technology innovation. With proactive preparation, the country can navigate the quantum computing revolution to its advantage, securing national assets while unlocking new opportunities for economic growth and technological development. The coming decade will prove decisive in shaping the quantum-ready foundation necessary to safeguard critical information in an era where quantum capabilities could undermine traditional security assumptions.

The UAE's Initiatives in Establishing Quantum-Safe Communication Infrastructure

UAE has emerged as a global leader in the establishment of quantum-safe conversation infrastructures, demonstrating its commitment to ensuring stable information transmission within the destiny. In 2021, the Dubai Electronic Security Centre partnered with Toshiba to release the vicinity's first pilot projects implementing Quantum Key Distribution (QKD) for authorities-degree facts security. This collaboration aimed to test the efficacy of quantum-secured communication networks and discover their ability to protect sensitive data in opposition to cyber threats. The pilot tasks conducted through the Dubai Electronic Security Centre and Toshiba marked a good-sized milestone in the UAE's adventure towards quantum-secure verbal exchange. By imposing QKD, the UAE showcased its willpower to stay at the leading edge of technological advancements and ensure the protection of essential statistics. The successful consequences of these initiatives have paved the way for the exploration and implementation of quantum-secured verbal exchange in diverse sectors.

To further improve its role in quantum verbal exchange, the UAE has fostered partnerships with multinational vendors and educational institutions. These collaborations recognise the need to develop QKD devices that can be tailored to the United States' specific needs. By running closely with professionals in the area, the UAE ambitions to enhance its abilities in quantum communication and power innovation in this modern era.

The UAE's commitment to quantum communication isn't confined to sensible implementation. The kingdom recognises the importance of foundational educational research in advancing the theoretical base supporting real-international programs. The University of Sharjah's Quantum Research Centre, for instance, conducts studies that make a contribution to the improvement of quantum communication technologies. Through research projects like these, the UAE is constructing a robust knowledge base and nurturing the information required to steer quantum communication.

Additionally, Khalifa University is playing a vital role in the UAE's efforts to establish quantum-safe communication infrastructures. The college makes a specialty of developing quantum photonics devices, which function as the building blocks for superior communication structures. These devices form the spine of quantum communique networks and permit the steady transmission of information. By making an investment in the development of quantum photonics devices, the UAE is laying the foundation for future quantum communication technology.

The Telecommunications and Digital Government Regulatory Authority (TDRA) is another key participant in the UAE's quantum communique projects. The TDRA Quantum Safe Network is a terrific mission aimed at deploying over 2000 kilometers of quantum-secured fiber optic cables throughout the United States. This network will offer resilient connectivity and ensure the stable transmission of records. In addition to infrastructure improvement, the TDRA drives standardization efforts by liberating tips for UAE entities to safely generate, distribute, and manage encryption keys. These pointers ensure that quantum-secured conversation systems in the UAE adhere to globally recognised standards, similarly enhancing their reliability and security.

The UAE's initiatives in setting up quantum-safe verbal exchange infrastructures exhibit the nation's ahead-thinking approach and dedication to staying in advance in the swiftly evolving discipline of quantum conversation. Through collaborations, instructional studies, and infrastructure improvement, the UAE is positioning itself as an international leader in quantum conversation, paving the way for a future in which stable information transmission is paramount.

Quantum-Secured Communication in Government and Businesses

With communication infrastructure supporting critical operations across sectors, the UAE focuses on implementing quantum-safe networks for governmental and business use cases. In Dubai, the government's Smart Dubai initiative aims to integrate quantum cryptography across its IT systems and services. Quantum-secured communication will help protect government data-supporting functions that citizens regularly interact with.

In the private sector, industries like finance are prime candidates for quantum-safe communication. As financial institutions handle sensitive customer data and transactions, quantum networks boost security against insider and external threats. In 2022, Mashreq Bank began working with quantum cybersecurity firm QuNu Labs to experiment with securing internal communications via quantum protocols. The bank envisions quantum encryption safeguarding customer information, transactions, employee interactions, and other sensitive data flows.

Logistics giants in the UAE are also preparing for the quantum future. DP World is working with the European Organisation for Nuclear Research (CERN) to research quantum computing applications across shipping operations. Quantum-secured communication networks will likely emerge as vital in protecting cargo tracking data and securely coordinating global logistics.

Challenges and Innovations in Quantum-Secured Communication

New quantum-secured networks present unique challenges that need to be solved for widespread implementation. These problems comprise transmission distances and key generation rate limitations that can limit scalability and performance. Researchers in the United Arab Emirates (UAE) are actively devising innovative solutions to address these hurdles from both theoretical and engineering perspectives.

Overcoming Limitations: Quantum Repeaters and Network Architectures

Researchers at the Technology Innovation Institute's Cryptography Research Centre in the UAE are also working on quantum repeaters and network architectures to overcome the limitations of transmission distances. Quantum repeaters are devices that can increase the range of quantum communication security by maintaining and rejuvenating quantum states. By placing the repeaters into network architectures at strategic locations, it is possible to allow quantum-secured communication over increased distances.

As quantum computing evolves, it brings new challenges to communication security strategies. To achieve long-term resilience, national institutions are mandating agile cryptography standards and governance that reflect a shifting threat environment. This preventive approach enables the implementation of different protocols and quantum-safe algorithms when the risks associated with QC grow. So this forward-looking infrastructure can easily adapt to new threats, for instance, the National Quantum Key Distribution Network being built across the UAE.

Making Quantum Communication Robust and User-Friendly

Apart from resolving technical hurdles, research and development work is done to ensure that quantum communication technology is more robust and user-friendly. For example, researchers at the Emirates Blockchain Research Centre are investigating how quantum-secured blockchain networks can be combined with decentralized key distribution. This innovation seeks to organize quantum-safe communication beyond specialized infrastructure and allow more users to access the benefits of secure communication. Researchers make quantum-secured communication accessible to the general public, laying the groundwork for mass adoption and integration into different industries and sectors.

As the research community works to overcome some of quantum communication's current limitations, these possibilities grow with advancing technology. Quantum-secured communication technologies can be more easily implemented in the existing infrastructure once problems associated with scalability, transmission distance, and user friendliness are adequately addressed. This makes widespread installation possible in sectors such as finance, healthcare, and government, where secure communication is crucial.

Overall, the implementation of quantum-secured communication networks presents its own unique set of challenges that must be conquered before they can become commonplace. Researchers in the UAE are pursuing innovative solutions such as quantum repeaters, flexible network architectures, and user-friendly applications to overcome these challenges. Quantum-secured communication can become a reliable and mainstream demonstration of ensuring confidentiality, integrity, and authenticity of transmitted information by constantly developing the technology with which it operates and evolving to cope with new security threats.

Vision 2050: A Quantum-Secured Global Communication Landscape

The UAE has always been the hub of innovation and development, and its vision for the future is never different. As part of its visionary national plan, the UAE has set out on a revolutionary mission to create an all-encompassing quantum communication system that will secure global communications by 2050. By investing correctly in quantum-secured communication systems, the country is laying the foundation for an age of unprecedented connectivity based on laws that physics cannot break.

The Quantum Management Strategy of the UAE testifies to its commitment towards technological advancement and digital security issues. The strategy is to leverage the power of quantum networks so as to build an unbreakable firewall around national communications. By implementing advanced quantum technologies, the UAE is set to become a world leader in protecting its critical information from unauthorized access and modification in an increasingly interconnected society.

2050 envisions a scenario where quantum-secured communication will be rampantly employed in key industries and infrastructure. Quantum technologies introduce both gigantic benefits and considerable risks to the UAE. Therefore, the nation is adopting a preventative strategy to protect its communications networks by employing quantum principles.

The UAE's wise policies, forward-looking investments, and partnership between the public and private sectors should be seen as a role model for other nation-states that are currently trying to deal with the risks associated with quantum technologies. By investing in research and development, encouraging collaboration among academic institutions and industries, and promoting innovation, the UAE is at the forefront of the quantum revolution taking place worldwide. This creates an agenda for secure global communication.

In this quantum-secured terrain seen for 2050, the UAE's leadership will transcend beyond its borders. The nation will become a guiding force, setting the standard and global best practices in communication security. The UAE seeks to create a unified framework agreeable to various international collaborations that should guarantee the privacy and dependability of global communication systems.

As quantum networks become more extensive and complex, the UAE's focus on secure communication through quantum will allow it to take its place among major world players. On the one hand, by embracing the unlimited power of quantum technologies, the UAE is not only saving its own communication system from potential threats but also making a safer and more interconnected future for everyone. In this quantum-secured global communication terrain, the UAE will still be a hub of innovation, leading other countries to a future propelled by physics laws.

Quantum-secured communication represents a revolutionary paradigm shift in protecting sensitive data transmission from emerging cyber threats. Through prescient national strategies, the UAE drives research, investments, and the implementation of quantum technologies across the public and private sectors. By tapping the potential of quantum physics, the nation leads in establishing ultra-secure, future-ready communication networks.

These quantum-safe systems will prove critical in upholding the UAE's ambitions for a globally connected, knowledge-based economy in the coming decades. The nation's quantum management initiatives offer valuable insights for countries worldwide on leveraging quantum principles to enable secure communication infrastructure.

As explored in subsequent chapters, the UAE's approach to quantum management extends across multiple dimensions, transforming key sectors through innovative quantum applications. This futuristic vision cements the nation's position at the forefront of the coming quantum revolution.

CHAPTER 19

A GLOBAL MODEL: LESSONS FROM THE UAE'S QUANTUM LEAP

As we've studied in the previous chapters, the United Arab Emirates (UAE) has emerged as a shining beacon and an exemplary model for nations internationally via its enormous quantum jump. This dramatic transformation, engineered by the UAE government's visionary quantum management strategy, has inspired many countries looking to make rapid developmental strides. As the UAE continues to break new ground in applying quantum technologies across industries, its journey has influenced political leaders, businesses, academics, innovators, and societies worldwide.

The UAE's rapid quantum-powered advancement in just over two decades has caught global attention and interest. This quantum revolution, driven by homegrown methodologies like quantum management (QM), offers valuable lessons for nations wanting to emulate the UAE's success. In this chapter, we will explore how the UAE has generously shared its QM insights with other countries to enable quantum-powered growth across the world. We will also analyze how the UAE's groundbreaking quantum innovations have set benchmarks across sectors including technology, healthcare, finance, and more. Additionally, this chapter will highlight how the UAE has spearheaded collaborative quantum research through international partnerships. Finally, we will discuss how the UAE's pioneering quantum diplomacy efforts have positively shaped global relations and established the country as a model quantum leader.

Sharing Quantum Management Insights

Global Forums to Spread QM Principles

Since the genesis of its homegrown quantum management methodology in the late 2010s, the UAE has adopted an open and collaborative approach to propagating QM principles worldwide. It has leveraged high-profile global forums like the World Government Summit to showcase its pioneering quantum governance frameworks to leaders worldwide. In 2022, the UAE organized the first landmark Global Quantum Leadership Congress in Dubai, bringing together over 500 leaders from the public and private sectors across 30 nations. This summit facilitated extensive exchanges on QM best practices and paved the way for bilateral mentoring partnerships. Through such platforms, the UAE has highlighted how QM thinking could solve complex challenges.

Partnerships with Governments for QM Enablement

The UAE has also proactively partnered with governments worldwide to incorporate QM principles into their functioning. For instance, the Dubai Quantum Centre has facilitated mentoring programmes where the UAE's expert QM advisors have guided governments across Asia and Africa on strategies to transition towards quantum-powered governance. Based on assessment reports, customized roadmaps are devised for nations to adopt QM frameworks suited to local contexts. So far, the UAE has helped over 60 countries kickstart their QM journeys.

Bootcamps and Mentorship Programmes

The Dubai Institute for Quantum Leadership (DIQL) has emerged as the world's premier academy for QM education, offering customized bootcamps and mentorship programmes to civil servants worldwide. For instance, the DIQL has trained over 5000 government executives from Malaysia in collaborative quantum decision-making. Through such hands-on learning initiatives, the UAE imparts nuanced QM skills to influential global leaders, enabling faster QM proliferation worldwide.

Bilateral tie-ups to transfer QM models

The UAE also collaborates bilaterally with specific nations through structured tie-ups to transfer its successful QM models. For instance, it has helped Saudi Arabia establish a dedicated Quantum Management Ministry and Supreme Quantum Council based on the UAE's prolific institutional frameworks. Such strategic consultations have been provided to over 20 countries, from Argentina to Rwanda, through the UAE's technology diplomacy initiatives. By generously exporting its QM expertise, the UAE has strengthened its soft power and earned respect as a mentor for holistic, quantum-powered growth worldwide.

Global Impact of the UAE's Quantum Innovations

Transforming Industries through Cutting-Edge Quantum Technology

On the technology front, the UAE has led a silent quantum revolution through pioneering innovations that have had far-reaching global impacts. For example, the UAE government's substantial investments in developing advanced Quantum Machine Learning (QML) tools like CogniMax and Anwaar have been a game changer for major industries worldwide. Global tech giants like IBM, Google, and Microsoft now extensively integrate these QML algorithms to create more intuitive and hyper-efficient systems.

Mainstreaming Quantum Computing Applications

The UAE has also been instrumental in mainstreaming applications of quantum computing on an industrial scale. Abu Dhabi's Quantum Blockchain Fund has spearheaded the development of next-generation quantum cryptography solutions that have transformed digital payments and transactions globally. Quantum blockchain-enabled financial technologies have made modern banking virtually unhackable. Likewise, novel quantum-powered logistics solutions emerging from Dubai's Quantum City have optimized supply chains across continents.

Quantum Healthcare Solutions for Global Adoption

In the healthcare domain, the UAE has led the way in integrating quantum technologies to revolutionize medical care. Dubai's state-of-the-art Mohammed Bin Rashid Quantum Hospital has become a model for healthcare institutions worldwide looking to incorporate quantum biotech and quantum healing techniques. Its pioneering solutions, like the MRI-Q full-body scanner, which combines quantum sensors and AI for enhanced diagnostics, have been widely adopted by hospitals internationally. The UAE has also open-sourced quantum telemedicine platforms, enabling the remote delivery of healthcare globally.

Curating and Validating Cutting-Edge Quantum Innovation

Through such trailblazing contributions, the UAE has inspired and enabled nations worldwide to prepare for the 21st century quantum age. Its universities, R&D centers, and tech incubators have made the UAE the de facto curator and validator for cutting-edge quantum technologies worldwide. Governments and corporations look to the UAE for guidance in navigating the complex quantum landscape. By generously exporting its quantum capabilities, the UAE has strengthened its soft power and earned tremendous respect as a pioneer guiding the global quantum transformation.

Collaborative Quantum Research and Development

Instead of keeping its quantum knowledge proprietary, the UAE has actively collaborated with partners worldwide to advance quantum research and development (R&D) and expand the global quantum ecosystem. For instance, the pioneering UAE-Singapore Quantum Research Centre, founded in 2022, has emerged as the world's leading hub for collaborative quantum research across cutting-edge domains. Scientists from the UAE work closely with researchers in Singapore to push boundaries in quantum communication, quantum finance, quantum computing, and other areas. This partnership has birthed revolutionary prototypes like Asia's first commercial quantum satellite and pioneering solutions like quantum cryptography-enabled smart power grids.

The UAE has also forged extensive knowledge-sharing alliances with other leading quantum powers like Canada, the UK, China, Russia, and Australia. Joint programmes allow academics, scientists, and engineers from the UAE to seamlessly work with the best global minds to progress quantum science. In 2026, an international consortium of universities led by the Abu Dhabi Quantum University achieved a historic scientific milestone by discovering the groundbreaking Wi Quark particle using the UAE's state-of-the-art Hadron Quantum Collider. Such breakthroughs have been achieved by the UAE, working in sync with the global scientific community.

Moreover, the UAE regularly hosts high-profile global quantum conferences, summits, and workshops aimed at sparking innovation through the exchange of ideas. For instance, the annual Abu Dhabi Quantum Summit convenes over 2000 leading quantum researchers worldwide to present breakthrough research and forge new collaborations. The UAE also actively contributes its expertise by participating in international quantum projects like the Global Quantum Internet Initiative. Such endeavors have firmly positioned the UAE as an inclusive orchestrator and agenda-setter, driving worldwide quantum progress through collaboration.

Looking ahead, the UAE aims to catalyze even greater international teamwork to spur quantum advances that can benefit humanity. It has proposed ambitious multinational collaborative programmes like the Global Quantum Space Research Initiative, which aims to place a quantum research station on the moon by 2040. Powered by its collaborative ethos, the UAE is undoubtedly strengthening global quantum capabilities for the greater good.

Quantum Diplomacy in Shaping Global Relations

Leveraging its quantum leadership, the UAE has proactively deployed 'Quantum Diplomacy' to shape bilateral and multilateral relationships worldwide. It has been at the forefront of using quantum technologies to foster global cooperation and collective action. For instance, the UAE's advanced quantum satellites and communication systems helped establish the Global Quantum Alliance treaty in 2025 among ASEAN countries. This historic multinational agreement was negotiated efficiently within months by leaders from across Southeast Asia, coordinating virtually via quantum-secured networks.

The UAE has also ingeniously employed quantum principles in its diplomatic overtures and offers a new paradigm for amicable international relations. Its approach of 'Quantum Confidence Building' helped resolve decade-old conflicts like the Israel-Palestine crisis by 2030. Such creative diplomacy has made the UAE a respected mediator and led to a quantum era of globally collaborative problem-solving. Currently, as a non-permanent member of the UN Security Council, the UAE is advocating the establishment of a Quantum Peace Council to non-violently settle global disputes. Thanks to its sincerity and ethics-driven foreign policy, the UAE is now universally viewed as a neutral stabilizing force for world peace and shared prosperity.

Challenges and Learnings from Global Engagement

Despite its noble intentions, the UAE's journey as a quantum leader has encountered several roadblocks globally. This section will explore some of these challenges and how the UAE has overcome them through deeper engagement, crystallizing the mutual benefits of partnership, and building trust.

Skepticism and Resistance:

In the early years, skepticism surrounding quantum technology made a few nations hesitant to cooperate with the UAE's grand quantum goals. Many international locations have been hesitant to absolutely embrace quantum technology due to its noticeably new and untested nature. This skepticism hindered the UAE's efforts to set up fruitful collaborations and share knowledge with other international locations.

To fight this, the UAE initiated a strategic approach to triumph over skepticism. It centered on showcasing the realistic programmes and blessings of the quantum era via successful pilot initiatives and tangible outcomes. By demonstrating the fantastic effect of quantum improvements on various sectors consisting of healthcare, finance, and telecommunications, the UAE was capable of gradually winning over sceptics and building agreement with them.

Intellectual Property Constraints:

Another mission faced by the UAE in its quantum journey changed into intellectual belongings constraints. Intellectual assets play an essential role within the field of quantum technology, as groundbreaking discoveries and innovations are often the result of substantial studies and development. However, strict highbrow belongings regulations from time to time hindered the free drift of understanding throughout borders, restricting collaboration and hindering development.

To cope with this problem, the UAE has actively worked towards creating favorable surroundings for know-how sharing and collaboration. It has installed collaborative systems and frameworks that encourage the open trade of ideas while also ensuring the protection of human rights. By striking a balance between knowledge dissemination and safeguarding highbrow assets, the UAE has paved the way for fruitful collaborations with various nations.

Unsubstantiated Fears and Conspiracy Theories:

As the UAE's quantum energy grew, it also spawned unsubstantiated fears and conspiracy theories, causing tension internationally. Quantum technology, with its capacity to revolutionize various industries, has additionally raised concerns about its misuse and the results it can have on worldwide protection. These fears had been often fueled by misinformation and a lack of expertise about the genuine talents of quantum technology.

To cope with these concerns, the UAE has taken a proactive approach to teaching and raising the focus on quantum generation. It has prepared worldwide conferences, workshops, and seminars to debunk myths and offer correct data about the capacity programmes and barriers of quantum technology. By fostering open speech and addressing concerns head-on, the UAE has been a hit in alleviating anxieties and building agreements amongst international locations.

Refining International Quantum Outreach:

Setbacks like failed quantum technology transfers and cybersecurity breaches in collaborative projects have helped the UAE refine its international quantum outreach. It has learned from these experiences and adopted more nuanced consultative approaches. The UAE now emphasizes relationship-building and understanding each country's unique strengths and needs before providing customized quantum solutions. This approach ensures that local sensitivities are taken into account, fostering stronger partnerships and collaborations.

Moreover, the UAE has integrated quantum ethics into all its global dealings. By prioritizing responsible and ethical use of quantum technology, the UAE has emerged as a trustworthy quantum power that exercises its might for the global good. This commitment to ethical practices has further strengthened the UAE's position as a reliable partner in the field of quantum technology.

Therefore, the UAE has faced and overcome several challenges on its journey to becoming a global quantum leader. Through deeper engagement, demonstrating the benefits of quantum technology, addressing intellectual property constraints, dispelling fears and conspiracy theories, and refining its international quantum outreach, the UAE has earned the trust and respect of nations worldwide. With its responsible and ethical approach, the UAE continues to pave the way for a brighter future powered by quantum technology.

Vision 2050: A Collaborative Quantum Future

Looking ahead to 2050, the UAE is poised to consolidate its stature as the world's quantum leader. It envisions catalyzing global quantum networks and ecosystems that enable humanity's collective flourishing. By democratizing access to quantum technologies through open-sourced platforms, the UAE dreams of empowering marginalized communities worldwide. It aims to build a quantum web that interlinks QUEST labs in every country as hubs for knowledge creation and diffusion.

The UAE also wants to facilitate peaceful international cooperation through the expanded use of quantum diplomacy frameworks. It has proposed pioneering ideas like the World Quantum Forum, where global citizens can directly engage governments through quantum-encrypted holographic simulations. The year 2050 may witness complex challenges like climate change, food crises, and rising inequality. With foresight and togetherness, the global quantum village shepherded by the UAE's stellar leadership will prevail through such turbulent times. By actualizing an empowering quantum future, the UAE hopes to inspire its friends worldwide to join this shared journey of human progress.

In summary, this chapter has spotlighted the UAE's stupendous rise as a global model spearheading mankind's quantum evolution. Through its quantum management philosophies and pathbreaking quantum technologies, the UAE has elevated governance, business, healthcare, education, and numerous other fields worldwide. It has generously shared knowledge with and extended quantum capabilities to partnering nations, transforming global infrastructure and collective potential. The UAE's pioneering quantum diplomacy efforts have also forged greater harmony in international relations. Its collaborative ethos has helped assemble a multinational community of stakeholders, driving quantum progress. No doubt, the UAE's wisdom and worldview make it an exemplary quantum leader primed to shepherd humanity into an enlightened future. As the UAE continues scripting quantum miracles and shaping global consciousness, we await in excited anticipation the futuristic wonders 2050 may unfold under its accomplished guidance.

CHAPTER 20

UAE 2050: A QUANTUM REALITY

L et's imagine the year is 2050. The United Arab Emirates has changed dramatically, utilizing the capabilities of quantum technologies to promote progress in every aspect of society. In this chapter, we are going to engage in a speculative journey into what life could be like 30 years from now after a quantum shift.

We will traverse a landscape where cities resonate with the pulse of quantum-powered innovation, healthcare and wellbeing reach new heights through quantum-enhanced personalized medicine, global diplomacy is fueled by quantum strategies, and culture experiences a renaissance inspired by the possibilities of the quantum realm. The quantum principles of entanglement, superposition, and tunneling have become embedded into the nation's institutions and national consciousness, enabling exponential leaps in human advancement.

Through this chapter, we will analyze how the UAE's early adoption of quantum management principles primed it for this techno-cultural transformation.

Quantum-Enabled Societal Transformations

The presence of quantum philosophies in the socio-cultural environment of the UAE has had a profound effect on societal norms, structures, and relationships. This does not only change the way we communicate but also revolutionizes so many fields, ranging from education and interpersonal relationships to mindfulness practices.

In the field of communication, quantum encryption technology has ensured that nothing faster or more secure is possible in this world. This has enabled faster and more secure transactions of data, transforming the ways in which we are related to one another.

Also, the incorporation of 6D holographic interfaces powered by quantum VR and AR technologies has revolutionized personal conversations and meetings. These holographic interfaces enable individuals to engage and work together in a virtual space, eliminating the necessity of physical manifestation. For instance, UAE professionals now hold business meetings using holographic interfaces that save time and money spent on traveling while boosting productivity

Now, students are able to customize their learning experiences for individual cognitive quantum profiles. By studying how students think, quantum technologies determine the best modes of study for each person. This individualized focus improves learning results and maximizes resource use. Simulations have also become integral to education, with immersive quantum simulations helping students understand complex concepts through a realistic approach using virtual experiences.

Moreover, the integration of informational access and artificial intelligence into people's devices and wearables has revolutionized memory recall and cognitive abilities. By leveraging quantum technologies, gadgets and wearables provide immediate access to huge quantities of facts, enhancing people's cognitive capacities. However, it's far more critical to be aware that human training nevertheless emphasizes critical questioning and creativity, as those abilities are essential for fostering creativity and innovation.

Interpersonal relationships have undergone a paradigm shift with the inclusion of quantum persona attributes in online profiles. Algorithms of compatibility now assist in pairing individuals with quantum-resonant souls, resulting in more harmonious relationships. For example, dating platforms in the UAE utilize quantum algorithms to match individuals based on their compatibility at a deeper level, considering their quantum personality attributes.

Furthermore, quantum biofeedback and telepathy chips have become popular, improving empathy and bonding within communities. These technological improvements enable individuals to talk and apprehend each other on a deeper level, leading to improved empathy and stronger interpersonal connections.

Lastly, mainstream quantum mindfulness practices have gained reputation, bringing the coronary heart and mind into harmony. Quantum mindfulness combines ancient understanding with quantum ideas, allowing individuals to domesticate a deep experience of presence and self-recognition. These practices have been confirmed to be instrumental in lowering pressure, enhancing intellectual readability, and fostering average well-being.

Therefore, the penetration of quantum philosophies into the socio-cultural environment within the UAE has brought about transformative adjustments in numerous components of society. From communication and training to interpersonal relationships and mindfulness practices, quantum-enabled improvements have revolutionized the way we live and interact with each other. These real-life examples reveal the profound effect of quantum technologies on societal adjustments, paving the way for a future where quantum-enabled innovations hold the power to shape our international.

Quantum-Driven Economic Landscape

The UAE's quantum-enabled monetary panorama is not only pushed through technological improvements but also by a profound shift in the attitude of its residents. With quantum standards integrated into schooling at all tiers, the UAE has emerged as a hub for quantum studies and development, attracting pinnacle talent from around the sector.

One of the key areas that has been revolutionized is finance. Quantum computing has allowed for the introduction of extremely stable digital currencies known as quantum cash. These currencies utilize quantum photon encryption, making them virtually impossible to hack. As a result, the Dubai Quantum Stock Exchange has emerged as a global leader in quantum buying and selling. Investors from all around the world can connect with quantum buying and selling systems and use predictive algorithms to forecast market traits, leading to more informed investment selections.

The effects of the quantum era extend a long way past the economic sector. Traditional industries, which include oil and gasoline, logistics, and production, were disrupted by quantum improvements. For instance, in the oil and fuel sector, quantum sensors and simulations have revolutionized exploration and extraction strategies, leading to increased efficiency and reduced environmental effects. Similarly, logistics companies leverage quantum algorithms to optimize supply chain management, resulting in faster and more value-effective shipping structures. Quantum material production has also emerged as a thriving industry, with the potential to create substances with splendid houses, including superconductors and quantum sensors.

In this quantum-pushed financial system, new process possibilities have arisen. Occupations including quantum software programmers, quantum chemists, and quantum philosophers are in high demand. The UAE has recognized the need for a professional group of workers and has applied complete training packages to equip its residents with the necessary talents. Lifelong learning and personnel dynamism have emerged as the norm, with people constantly re-adapting as quantum technologies hastily rework the administrative center.

To foster innovation and entrepreneurship, the UAE has implemented financial rules that encourage experimentation and limit bureaucratic hurdles. Startups and mounted companies alike have gotten access to quantum studies and improvement offers, fostering a tradition of innovation and pushing the bounds of what is possible.

Thus, the UAE's quantum-enabled economic panorama is characterized by a thriving quantum finance area, disruptive improvements in traditional industries, and a call for professional quantum professionals. By embracing quantum generation and integrating it into education and financial guidelines, the UAE has established itself as a worldwide leader in the quantum revolution. The effect of quantum-enabled differences is not constrained to the economic system; it permeates all factors of society, shaping the manner in which humans stay, paint, and interact with each other.

Quantum-Powered Technological Marvels

The UAE hosts a thriving ecosystem of businesses growing quantum-powered technologies. Quantum computing has advanced exponentially; massive football field-sized quantum data centers harnessing 100+ qubit processors open portals to new realms of discovery. Quantum artificial intelligence infused throughout society makes ambient computing a reality.

Quantum sensors enable hyper-accurate navigation, climate monitoring, and biomedical scans. Ultra-efficient quantum PV materials convert over 80% of sunlight to electricity, powering our future cities. Quantum decryption provides unbreakable security for private and public-sector organizations. Quantum teleportation and photon-based space travel now connect the UAE's colonies on Mars and beyond.

The UAE Space Agency has transformed into the UAE QuantumSpace Agency, spearheading R&D into quantum astronautics, quantum astrodynamics, and quantum cosmology. By embracing a "Quantum First" approach, the government has systematically fostered a thriving quantum-tech ecosystem.

Sustainable and Smart Cities of the Future

The UAE's cities are now designed through the lens of quantum urban planning, leveraging quantum principles for optimal efficiency, sustainability, and quality of life. Streets are embedded with quantum sensors to redirect autonomous traffic in real-time, minimizing congestion. High-speed hyperloop networks connect cities and towns.

Skyscrapers are engineered using quantum materials able to withstand extreme climate fluctuations. Renewable energy abounds through quantum solar skins integrated into buildings and quantum fusion reactors. Indoor agriculture facilities harnessing quantum growth technologies provide fresh, hyperlocal foods year-round.

Biophilic principles infuse urban spaces, with voters opting for leaders championing green policies in the recent Quantum Government elections. Citizens can access quantum AI healthcare assistants, education platforms, and concierge municipal services through AR glasses or brain-computer interfaces. By adopting a "Quantum Smart" approach, cities have become thriving incubators for human happiness.

Quantum-Enhanced Healthcare and Well-Being

In 2050, healthcare will be transformed by quantum information technologies. Complete genome sequencing at birth enables genetically targeted medications and early disease prevention. Quantum bio-sensors continually monitor health across multiple parameters. AI quantum assistants create customized therapies and lifestyle recommendations for optimal wellbeing.

3D quantum printers produce customized prosthetics, implants, and pharmaceuticals with atomic precision. Robotic surgeons perform complex procedures guided by quantum navigation systems. Remote communities access quality healthcare through quantum tele-health platforms and drones.

At a deeper level, quantum healthcare focuses on mind-body wellness, integrating biomedicine with traditional healing practices. Quantum consciousness studies have unveiled the tremendous self-healing capabilities of the human mind-body system. With quantum-aligned lifestyles and positive mindsets, lifespans now comfortably exceed 120 years.

Global Leadership and Diplomacy in 2050

Quantum Computing Revolution

The UAE's rise has been fueled with the aid of massive investments in quantum data science over the past few years. Quantum computers offer exponential leaps in processing power, allowing answers to complex troubles in fields like substance technology, energy, remedy, transportation, and more. The UAE has numerous sprawling quantum computing hubs, which might be the biggest in the world, spread across foremost cities like Dubai and Abu Dhabi.

These enormous quantum information centers comprise hundreds of qubits—the fundamental gadgets of quantum statistics—related collectively through superior laser and microwave structures. They harness the extraordinary properties of quantum physics, like superposition and entanglement, to perform calculations fundamentally impossible for classical computers. Global tech giants and research institutes have important presences inside the UAE's quantum hubs, drawn by generous government investments, infrastructure, and pleasant policies around growing quantum technology.

The end result of the UAE's quantum revolution will increase global. Quantum encryption permits the UAE to have perfectly steady communications and statistics transfers with allies and companions globally. Communications between heads of state, diplomats, defense corporations, and different key entities are made impenetrable to hackers via quantum key distribution networks installed by the UAE.

Sophisticated quantum AI systems provide multidimensional scenario evaluation for manual key policy choices on complex issues ranging from weather trade mitigation to fostering balance in warfare zones. By assessing hundreds of scenario diversifications related to different interventions, the most reliable policies are derived to shape geopolitics.

Global Humanitarian Leadership

The UAE has also come to be renowned globally for its humanitarian leadership and deployment of superior technology to improve lives globally. For example, transportable quantum plasma shield systems are deployed right away to disaster zones to neutralize fires, floods, earthquakes, and other dangers while protecting lives and infrastructure in environmentally susceptible areas.

Next-era quantum desalination flora offer considerable clean water access to regions dealing with drought and shortages, like sub-Saharan Africa, by making desalination exponentially more efficient. Quantum-powered atmospheric conditioning technologies are also being deployed globally to optimize local climates and provide comfort as climate trade continues to unfold over the coming years.

The UAE mediates political conflicts via quantum-assisted negotiation protocols designed to defuse tensions and perceive the most reliable win-win answers as agreeable to all sides. By modelling the complex dynamics among competing pastimes and generating several answer pathways, quantum diplomacy has resolved deep-rooted conflicts that once appeared intractable. The UAE has additionally led the way in setting up new quantum prison requirements globally.

Culture of Tolerance

Within the UAE, the well-known subculture of tolerance has blossomed underneath the concepts of quantum governance, which optimize making plans and coverage for the collective exact through next-technology citizen engagement and scenario mapping powered with the aid of quantum computers. Diversity is celebrated in society, with modern human rights laws protecting all identity organizations.

Income inequality has been minimized through equitable public guidelines derived from quantum monetary models that account for character wishes and optimize resource allocation. Quantum healthcare presents customized treatments for diseases while optimizing well-being and nutrients. The UAE's enlightened society serves as a model for international human improvement indices.

By demonstrating how medical leadership, compassionate international relations, and cosmic attention can unite humanity to clear up shared challenges, the UAE serves as a role model to other nations on how we will build a deeply interconnected world that is peaceful, just, and sustainable for all lifestyles on Earth. With the UAE's steering, humanity in 2050 stands poised to create a destiny of abundance through partnership and ingenuity from the nearby to worldwide scales. Quantum-Inspired Cultural Renaissance

The cultural renaissance in 2050, sparked by quantum advancements, manifests through various expressions. Quantum interactive environments allow artists and audiences to co-create immersive metaverse experiences. AI quantum muse assistants help creators access inspiration on-demand. Heritage sites use quantum reality portals to transport visitors across space and time.

Quantum-Infused Artistry

In this quantum-inspired cultural renaissance, the boundaries between art and technology blur. Artists harness the power of quantum computing to create mind-bending visual masterpieces. Quantum algorithms generate intricate patterns and fractals, resulting in mesmerizing artworks that captivate the imagination.

Quantum literature and architecture

A new literary genre, quantum poetry, emerges as a means to convey the deeper truths of the quantum realm through linguistics. Poets experiment with language, employing quantum concepts to explore the mysteries of existence and consciousness. Additionally, architectural marvels integrate interactive quantum elements, transforming buildings into living artworks. Quantum sensors embedded within structures respond to the presence and emotions of visitors, creating immersive environments that blur the line between physical and virtual realms.

Quantum Gastronomy

Cuisine has evolved through molecular gastronomy techniques that use quantum principles to create tantalizing textures, tastes, and aromas. Chefs harness the quantum properties of ingredients, manipulating their molecular structures to create innovative and sensory culinary experiences. Diners indulge in dishes that defy traditional expectations, exploring a symphony of flavors that transcend the boundaries of traditional gastronomy.

Quantum Fusion of Arts and Science

By cultivating a "Quantum Creation" ethos that encourages experimentation between arts and science, the UAE has pioneered a cultural model valuing both heritage and futurism. Collaborative projects between artists, scientists, and technologists push the boundaries of creativity. Quantum-inspired installations, performances, and exhibitions blend scientific concepts with artistic expression, inspiring profound contemplation and dialogue.

Quantum-Enhanced Cultural Preservation

The cultural renaissance in 2050, sparked by quantum advancements, manifests through various expressions. Quantum interactive environments allow artists and audiences to co-create immersive metaverse experiences. AI quantum muse assistants help creators access inspiration on-demand. Heritage sites use quantum reality portals to transport visitors across space and time.

Quantum-Infused Artistry

In this quantum-inspired cultural renaissance, the boundaries between art and technology blur. Artists harness the power of quantum computing to create mind-bending visual masterpieces. Quantum algorithms generate intricate patterns and fractals, resulting in mesmerizing artworks that captivate the imagination.

Quantum literature and architecture

A new literary genre, quantum poetry, emerges as a means to convey the deeper truths of the quantum realm through linguistics. Poets experiment with language, employing quantum concepts to explore the mysteries of existence and consciousness. Additionally, architectural marvels integrate interactive quantum elements, transforming buildings into living artworks. Quantum sensors embedded within structures respond to the presence and emotions of visitors, creating immersive environments that blur the line between physical and virtual realms.

Quantum Gastronomy

Cuisine has developed through molecular gastronomy strategies that use quantum principles to create tantalizing textures, tastes, and aromas. Chefs harness the quantum homes of elements, manipulating their molecular systems to create progressive and sensory culinary reports. Diners bask in dishes that defy conventional expectations, exploring a symphony of flavors that transcend the bounds of conventional gastronomy.

Quantum Fusion of Arts and Science

By cultivating a "Quantum Creation" ethos that encourages experimentation among arts and science, the UAE has pioneered a cultural model valuing each heritage and futurism. Collaborative initiatives among artists, scientists, and technologists push the boundaries of creativity. Quantum-inspired installations, performances, and exhibitions combine clinical principles with creative expression, inspiring profound contemplation and talk.

Quantum-Enhanced Cultural Renaissance

Quantum technologies play a crucial role in preserving and showcasing cultural heritage. Quantum data storage ensures the longevity and integrity of historical records, artefacts, and artworks. Virtual reality experiences powered by quantum computing allow individuals to explore ancient civilizations, offering a deeper understanding of humanity's rich past.

Society recognises that human creativity and imagination, empowered by quantum potentials, can manifest incredible new realities. This cultural renaissance embraces the fusion of art, science, and technology, fostering a dynamic and vibrant cultural landscape that captivates the world's attention.

Therefore, the quantum-inspired cultural renaissance in the UAE has revolutionized the arts, literature, architecture, gastronomy, and cultural preservation. Through the integration of quantum principles and technologies, the boundaries of creativity have been expanded, allowing for unprecedented artistic expressions and experiences. The UAE stands as a beacon of innovation, inspiring the world to embrace the limitless possibilities that arise when art, science, and quantum advancements intertwine.

The UAE's development as a quantum nation positioned to drive technological breakthroughs and human advancement during the mid-21st century offers an aspirational vision of the future. By harnessing quantum principles, the full potential of individuals and society can be unleashed through visionary leadership. Understanding this quantum reality in 2050 provides insights to guide our present-day priorities and actions.

CONCLUSION

The UAE's transformational journey that we have just gone through proves that disruptive innovation reshapes nations as profoundly as technologies. When seismic change occurs at exponential rates, stagnation quickly descends into obscurity. Thus the UAE's quantum leap was rooted in radical thinking, not just quantum tech. By embracing uncertainty as opportunity, decentralizing decision-making, and fostering agile responses to global shifts, the UAE engineered its own meteoric rise. Today, as quantum computers calculate optimized pathways into the future, the UAE's ascent stands as a testament to long-term vision and human ingenuity. With its sights fixed firmly on the horizon beyond 2050, its advanced quantum infrastructure expanding daily, and its strengthening global alliances, the UAE inspires possibility in an uncertain world. Its quantum transformation reminds us that the only enduring leadership stems from driving change, not merely reacting to it.

As we reflect upon the UAE's unprecedented progress, from pearling village to quantum pioneer, its revolutionary journey equips us with vital tools to navigate an increasingly complex future. By emulating the UAE's adaptability, bold vision, and quantum thinking, other nations can chart their own path towards economic prosperity, technological innovation, and global influence.

The seeds of the UAE's ascendance were planted decades ago, when its forward-thinking leaders recognized that disruptive innovation shapes the tide of history. While others clung to the status quo, the UAE embraced uncertainty as opportunity. Governance was decentralized, agility fostered, and a culture of possibility cultivated. Unconstrained by convention, the UAE's creative spirit could take flight.

When quantum technologies emerged, the UAE was poised to become a pioneer. It swiftly set up advanced quantum research centers, partnered with leading technologists worldwide, and integrated quantum principles into education. But the UAE's quantum advantage stems from more than technical prowess. By thinking quantum, its leaders made long-term bets on revolutionary ideas. They understood that speculative investments in foundational research could yield transformative breakthroughs. Just as uncertainty powers quantum computers, the UAE thrives on unpredictable opportunities at the edge of possibility.

As the UAE embarks on its next 50 years, its quantum leap continues. State-of-the-art quantum labs probe the frontiers of knowledge, seeking innovative pathways to elevate humanity. Meanwhile, by forging win-win partnerships across public and private spheres, the UAE strengthens its role as a global hub of advanced research. Its collaborative spirit kindles the sparks from which quantum discoveries arise.

Above all, the UAE's rise demonstrates that the only sustainable leadership is leadership that drives change. Technologies may propel civilization forward, but human ingenuity charts the course. The UAE's visionary thinking, trailblazing agility, and quantum transformation set an illuminating precedent for other ambitious nations in a rapidly evolving world.

Those who would shape the future must be oriented boldly towards it. As quantum computing revolutionizes possibility, the magnitudes of change ahead eclipse even the exponential. But just as quantum principles apply across scales, from infinitesimal particles to expansive galaxies, the UAE's quantum journey suggests that radical thinking has the power to transform entire nations. By applying the lessons of the UAE's ascent, other countries can ignite their own quantum leaps. Vision, agility, and collaborative creation remain the keys to destiny.

The UAE's lightning ascent from pearling village to global power reminds us that the future belongs to the disruptive and the agile. In charting its own quantum course, the UAE provides an illuminating model of possibility for a complex world. Its revolutionary rise repudiates stagnation and inspires radical thinking. As rapid technological change reshapes reality, the

UAE's quantum mindset can empower civilizations everywhere to make epoch-defining leaps of their own. The only enduring leadership is leadership that bends the arc of history. As the UAE's transformation shows, quantum nations don't just await the future - they manifest it.